Copyright's Highway

Also by Paul Goldstein

COPYRIGHT: PRINCIPLES, LAW AND PRACTICE

COPYRIGHT, PATENT, TRADEMARK AND RELATED STATE DOCTRINES:
CASES AND MATERIALS ON INTELLECTUAL PROPERTY LAW

CHANGING THE AMERICAN SCHOOLBOOK:
LAW, POLITICS AND TECHNOLOGY

Paul Goldstein

COPYRIGHT'S HIGHWAY

*

FROM GUTENBERG TO THE
CELESTIAL JUKEBOX

ⓦ HILL AND WANG

A division of Farrar, Straus and Giroux

New York

Copyright © 1994 by Paul Goldstein
All rights reserved
Printed in the United States of America
Published simultaneously in Canada by HarperCollins *Canada Ltd*
Designed by Fritz Metsch
First edition, 1994

LIBRARY OF CONGRESS CATALOGING-IN-PUBLICATION DATA
Goldstein, Paul.
Copyright's highway : from Gutenberg to the celestial jukebox /
Paul Goldstein.
p.   cm.
Includes index.
1. Copyright—United States.   I. Title.
KF2994.G654   1994   346.7304′82—dc20   [347.306482]   94-10831   CIP

To my family

Acknowledgments

Many of the people who were centrally involved in the events recounted in these pages took time from crowded schedules for lengthy interviews; I record my debt to them here and identify their particular contributions in the end notes. One of them, Arthur Greenbaum, deserves special thanks for his sustained and scholarly interest in the manuscript throughout.

This book also draws on the written record, and as so often in the past, I have depended heavily on the superb services of the Stanford Law Library staff—especially David Bridgman, Arline (Andy) Eisenberg, Paul Lomio, and Iris Wildman. Several students devoted uncountable hours, all in fine Stanford spirit, to research tasks ranging from organization of the book's hundreds of sources to tracking down references for accuracy: David Berger, Tony Reese, Michael Robinson, Debra Rosler, David Sanders, David Wagenfeld, Karen Wetherell, and Peter Wulsin have my deepest gratitude.

The book owes much to the wonderfully congenial environment for research and writing at the Stanford Law School, the product in no small part of Dean Paul Brest's unique

Acknowledgments

blend of intellectual grace and entrepreneurial steel. I particularly profited from conversations with my colleagues Ian Ayres, Bill Baxter, Bill Cohen, Robert Gordon, Joe Grundfest, Gerry Gunther, Mitch Polinsky, and Kathleen Sullivan. Gillian Hadfield reviewed the analysis of copyright's economic history with a sharp, critical eye, and Paul Geller—long my mentor in matters of foreign copyright—made many helpful suggestions on the book's treatment of international issues.

The book took its early shape from discussions with my friend and agent Martin Levin, who wisely—and accurately—predicted that my thoughts on copyright at the end of its writing would be very different from what they were at its beginning. The book was also helped at a critical point by astute suggestions from Arthur Rosenthal. The keen intelligence and deft hand of my editor, Elisabeth Sifton, touch every page; though invisible to the reader, they are memorable to me. I also owe a tremendous debt to my secretaries, Lynne Anderson and Moana Kutsche, who transcribed interviews and retyped what must have seemed unending drafts of manuscript tirelessly and with a warming good cheer that far transcended any job description or call of duty.

A generous grant from the John and Mary R. Markle Foundation supported early work on the book; I am indebted to the foundation and its president, Lloyd Morrisett, for their patient support. I am also grateful to the John M. Olin Program in Law and Economics at Stanford, the George Roberts Program in Law, Business and Corporate Governance, the Stanford Law and Technology Center, and the Claire and Michael Brown Estate for supplemental grants in support of research assistance and travel.

P.G.
Stanford, California
8 August 1994

Contents

Copyright's Highway

CHAPTER ONE

The Metaphysics of
Copyright

In late spring 1990, a major American music publisher entered into battle with a popular singing group over a handful of words and a few bars of music. In 1965, Acuff-Rose Music, the largest country music publisher in the world, had acquired rights to the song "Oh, Pretty Woman" from its writers, the celebrated pop star Roy Orbison and William Dees. Orbison's recording of the song was his last and biggest hit. Now, twenty-five years later, and without permission from Acuff-Rose, the controversial rap group 2 Live Crew had recorded its own version of the song on its latest album, sandwiching it between two other tracks, "Me So Horny" and "My Seven Bizzos." On June 18, 1990, Acuff-Rose filed suit in federal district court in Nashville, Tennessee, for infringement of its copyright.

What is copyright? From copyright law's beginnings close to three centuries ago, the term has meant just what it says: the right to make copies of a given work—at first it meant simply written work—and to stop others from making copies without one's permission. The first copyright laws aimed only at exact replications of printed work. The publishers of the eighteenth-century poet James Thomson's *The Seasons* regularly sued producers of unauthorized, or pirated, editions of the popular poem, since they controlled the copyright, obtained from Thomson. Starting in the mid-nineteenth century, copyright extended its reach. As the law evolved, copyright owners could stop the publication not only of exact knockoffs but also of imitations and adaptations: the translation into German of an English-language novel, a story's dramatization for the stage, an abridgment of a twelve-volume biography of George Washington.

And a rap parody of a poignant, popular lyric? One of copyright law's most bedeviling questions is how much one author can borrow from another before he becomes a copyright infringer. In an essay on "Literary Larceny," the English copyright scholar and barrister Augustine Birrell observed that "a particular leg of mutton is mine is capable of easy proof or disproof, *but how much of my book is mine* is a nice question." Getting the answer to that question right is important, because it is in the nature of creative work for one author to draw on the works of others. Drawing the line of copyright infringement too short will fail to give the original author his due, but extending it too far will make it hard for other writers to earn theirs.

Did 2 Live Crew cross the line when it borrowed from Orbison and Dees? The trial court found that while the group had copied some lyrics and music from "Oh, Pretty Woman," its rendition was very different. The song "starts out with the same lyrics as the original," but, the court added, "it quickly degenerates into a play on words, substituting predictable lyrics with shocking ones." Where Roy Orbison fantasizes about a beautiful woman he encounters on the street,

4

2 Live Crew had some very different fantasies in mind: a "big hairy woman," a "bald-headed woman," and a "two-timin'" woman.

The lawyers for 2 Live Crew understood that traditional copyright doctrine would judge their clients not by how much they had added to the Orbison-Dees original but by how much they had taken from it. Indeed, they effectively conceded that 2 Live Crew had infringed the copyright but for a single fact: the group's song was not an imitation but a parody, and parodies should be allowed to borrow more liberally than outright imitations. After all, how could a parodist make his point without conjuring up the original, and how could one conjure up the original without copying some of its content?

On January 14, 1991, the trial court handed down its decision. It agreed with 2 Live Crew's argument that parodies deserve elbow room, not only because the art of parody requires some degree of copying but also because it serves a larger cultural purpose—deflating cultural icons. The veteran folk singer Oscar Brand had testified for 2 Live Crew that African-American music commonly substitutes new words to "make fun of the 'white-bread' originals and the establishment." The court agreed. "2 Live Crew is an antiestablishment rap group and this song derisively demonstrates how bland and banal the Orbison song seems to them."

The dispute between Acuff-Rose and 2 Live Crew was just one of hundreds of copyright cases filed in 1990. Copyright cases run the gamut of popular culture, from songs, novels, and motion pictures to news stories, advertisements, photographs, and architecture. Copyright embraces more than art. Many cases involve instructional materials, scientific and scholarly texts, cookbooks—even computer programs. Some of these cases turn on broad principles like those invoked by 2 Live Crew. Others call for the interpretation of intricate statutory rules. Most turn on the answer to two questions: Has the defendant copied? Has he copied too much? All copyright cases have one fact in common: by telling authors how much they may lawfully borrow from earlier works and how much they must create on their own, copyright law indelibly colors the works it encompasses, whether news stories, stock market reports, scholarly articles, motion pictures, magazine pieces, or popular records.

Front-page copyright lawsuits like the *Pretty Woman* case have a clear effect on authors and their works. But that effect is usually felt far from the courtroom, in the corporate legal departments and private law offices to which executives in publishing companies, record companies, motion picture studios, and advertising agencies regularly turn for advice on how much can be taken from a copyrighted work without crossing the law's "No Trespassing" sign. Even insurance companies, which issue "errors and omissions" policies to protect publishers and film studios from the effects of adverse copyright decisions, have a say in what gets published and what does not.

All these decisions, whether made in the courts, legislatures, or private law offices, have a single result: when copyright gives control to one person, it extracts some measure of freedom to imitate from everyone else. What justifies this legally enforced exchange? One justification that artists and writers frequently advance is their privacy, the legally enforced seclusion they need to protect their early drafts, and even their correspondence, from public view. In 1986, the reclusive writer J. D. Salinger sought and obtained a copyright injunction to stop a biographer from publishing quotations from his private letters now housed in research libraries. Authors also look to copyright to preserve the integrity of their works. In 1976, the Monty Python comedy troupe went to court and used its copyrights to stop the ABC television network from broadcasting three of its programs in a version that had been truncated to accommodate commercial advertisements and network censors.

Mostly, though, copyright is about money. It can cost a lot to conceive, execute, produce, and market a creative work. The right to stop the copying of a work implies the power to allow it—at a price—and prospective copyright owners may rely on the hope of eventual copyright revenues to repay their initial investment. A songwriter assigns the copyright in a song to a music publisher, for example, in return for the promise of royalties paid on each copy sold or performed. The publisher sells a film company the right to use the song in a movie sound track, again in return for a share of the anticipated profits. Only the marketplace will determine whether a work has commercial value. But if the work has commercial value, copyright's aim is to put that value in the copyright owner's pocket.

Copyright concerns copies, not originals, and the money involved is usually a small price charged for each of the many copies made for people who want to share in a work, rather than a large price that an individual will pay to have for his own a work that is one-of-a-kind. When an object's value lies in its singularity and authenticity—a painting, for example, or an original manuscript in the author's hand—copyright has little effect on its value in the marketplace. But a novel can command a half-million-dollar advance against earnings for its author, because his royalties from the sales to hundreds of thousands of readers may at least equal that amount. The reason a painting by Jasper Johns will sell for millions is not that there is a market for copies but, on the contrary, that there is only one original. Even so, copyright can serve an artist's interest by enabling him to stop the selling or making of copies—posters, calendars—that might impair his work's singularity. Also, a recent amendment to the U.S. Copyright Act gives creators of fine art—works it defines to exist only in an original or in a limited edition—the right to prevent the distortion or mutilation of their works.

Copyright owners today wield their economic control with the deftness of a surgeon's scalpel. A publisher charges more for the initial hardcover edition of a novel than for the softcover edition that follows months or years later, not so much because the hardcover costs more to produce—though it does—as because the publisher knows that some readers will pay a premium to read a new book as soon as it is published, while other readers will trade immediate gratification for the lower price of a cheaper edition issued later. By adjusting its prices to these differing tastes, the publisher can earn a profit from each for both itself and the author. Motion picture companies first release their films to movie theaters, where the admission price is highest; six months later they sell videocassettes to video stores where viewers can rent the film for less; then comes home television pay-per-view, followed a year later by pay television; as much as three years later the film may appear "free" on network television. Without copyright, none of these commercial transactions would be possible.

Lawyers commonly classify copyright as an intellectual property law. And, indeed, copyright is related to other, more mundane forms of property. An author's right to ward off unauthorized copying of his work is much like a homeowner's right to keep trespassers off his land. But the "intellectual" part describes a distinctive attribute: copyright is not about protecting rights in a tangible object such as a piece of land or a leg of mutton. Copyright protects products of the human mind, the thoughts and expressions that one day may be found on the pages of a book and the next in a song or motion picture. It is hard to draw boundaries around such fugitive "properties." U.S. Justice Joseph Story observed this peculiarity more than a century and a half ago: "Copyrights approach, nearer than any other class of cases belonging to forensic discussions, to what may be called the metaphysics of the law, where the distinctions are, or at least may be, very subtle and refined, and, sometimes, almost evanescent."

A first step in understanding copyright law is to separate it from other intellectual property doctrines. In 1970, Alan Latman, a lawyer whose career soon became entwined with one of the pivotal chapters in the history of American copyright law, told a group of intellectual property specialists that "most people do not understand the differences between patents, trademarks, and copyrights. This applies to clients, other lawyers, and at times even judges. When I tell a general practitioner that I am a copyright lawyer, he immediately corrects me: 'You mean patents!' He then says: 'Well, anyway, as a patent lawyer, you can copyright a name for me, can't you?' " (The inside joke was that trademark law, not copyright law, protects names.)

Patent law's domain is invention and technology, the work that goes into creating new products, whether tractors, pharmaceuticals, or electric can openers. The United States Patent Act gives an inventor, or the company to which he has assigned his rights, the right to stop others from manufacturing, selling, or using an invention without the patent holder's permission. It originates in the same constitutional source as the Copyright Act—the clause in the U.S. Constitution empowering Congress to promote invention and authorship by granting inventors and authors "exclusive rights" in their "discoveries" and "writings." One reason it is so easy to confuse patents with copyrights is that Congress has read the term "writings" broadly, passing copyright laws that protect not only poems, novels, and plays but also such utilitarian objects as telephone directories, bookkeeping forms, and computer programs.

If copyright is the law of authorship and patent is the law of invention, trademark is the law of consumer marketing. Courts protect the terms Coca-Cola, McDonald's, and Kodak against imitation or unauthorized use, not because they represent creative or inventive leaps of the mind, but because they signify a single source of a product and a certain consistent level of quality to consumers. Trademark law aims to ensure that, whether in Portland, Maine, or Portland, Oregon, a traveler coming upon a fast-food restaurant with the familiar golden arches will get the same food offered in all other McDonald's restaurants. Just as copyright overlaps patents, it also overlaps trademarks. When the Walt Disney Company gets a court order stopping the publication of unauthorized cartoons featuring Mickey Mouse, it is not only because Mickey Mouse is a trademark, indicating Disney as its source, but also because Disney owns the copyright in the Mickey Mouse image.

Congress and the federal courts are not the only guarantors of intellectual property protection in the United States. It is state, not federal, law that protects trade secrets—the closeted technologies and formulas such as the much mythologized secret formula for Coca-Cola syrup—against theft by industrial spies and disaffected employees. Unfair competition laws enforced by state courts parallel federal trademark law, but without its formalities. If the Coca-Cola Company had failed to register its Coca-Cola mark in the Patent and Trademark Office in Washington, it could still fall back on state unfair competition law to protect it against anyone who sells soft drinks under a counterfeit Coca-Cola label.

None of these state or federal intellectual property categories is entirely rigid. Bubbling beneath all of them, including copyright, is the intuition that people should be able to hold on to the value of what they create, to reap where they have sown. When an intellectual property doctrine's traditional four corners will not readily accommodate this intuition, courts have pushed the doctrine's edges to give creators what they perceive to be their due. No one offered a T-shirt emblazoned with the famous Coca-Cola logo would think he was buying a soft drink. But the value—courts call it "good will"—that has accumulated around the Coca-Cola Company's mark over the years produces a predictable result: courts will prohibit the sale of the T-shirt as well as of any other marked product made without the company's consent.

Sometimes courts cannot stretch an existing intellectual property doctrine to protect new sources of commercial value. When in the 1960s famous athletes began lending their names to endorse sports equipment and rock stars began putting their faces on posters, these new pop celebrities wanted to be sure the right to use pictures of themselves was *their* right. Courts tried to fit this new claim—that unauthorized use of their images infringed their right—into traditional unfair competition and trademark law; but when these doctrines proved inadequate, they ultimately developed a new doctrine, the right of publicity, to embody the new idea about the commercial value of one's very own self. When a producer of portable toilets took the famous introductory line from *The Tonight Show* when Johnny Carson was its host, and proclaimed a new slogan for his product—"Here's Johnny" (the "World's Foremost Commodian")—a federal appeals court ruled that commercial use of the phrase violated Carson's right of publicity.

Plagiarism, which many people commonly think has to do with copyright, is not in fact a legal doctrine. True plagiarism is an ethical, not a legal, offense and is enforceable by academic authorities, not courts. Plagiarism occurs when someone—a hurried student, a neglectful professor, an unscrupulous writer—falsely claims someone else's words, whether copyrighted or not, as his own. Of course, if the plagiarized work is protected by copyright, the unauthorized reproduction is also a copyright infringement.

At the heart of all these doctrines, and certainly at the heart of copyright, is an intricate web of public and private interests. It is not at all easy to determine which is which. A journalist comes upon a newsworthy event. Can he stop others from reporting the facts that he observes, or does the very newsworthiness of the event mean the public should have free access to it? Should the legal answer turn on whether the news is passed from a bystander to his friends, or is relayed, at a price, to subscribers of a competing newspaper? Anyone who publicly distributes unauthorized videocassette copies of a motion picture is surely an infringer of copyright. But what of a VCR owner who copies the movie off his television set in the privacy of his home?

The clash between public and private interests in intellectual property becomes particularly vivid when a court is asked to establish a new legal doctrine for new kinds of copying. Bereft of guiding precedent, judges must return to first principles and independently evaluate the interests before them. The Supreme Court had to decide such a case in 1918, when the Associated Press wire service sued its competitor, the International News Service, for copying and selling AP news reports it had retrieved from AP bulletin boards and early editions of AP's member newspapers. Writing for the Court, Justice Mahlon Pitney framed the threshold question as "whether there is any property in news"—whether, that is, private rights can exist in public affairs.

Pitney and the Court recognized that copyright does not protect news. "It is not to be supposed that the framers of the Constitution, when they empowered Congress 'to promote the progress of science and useful arts, by securing for limited times to authors and inventors the exclusive right to their respective writings and discoveries' intended to confer upon one who might happen to be the first to report a historic event the exclusive right for any period to spread the knowledge of it." But the Court thought it unjust to let a competitor "reap where it has not sown," and so it fashioned a new intellectual property doctrine—misappropriation—to protect the Associated Press. "The right of the purchaser of a single newspaper to spread knowledge of its contents gratuitously, for any legitimate purpose not unreasonably interfering with complainant's right to make merchandise of it, may be admitted; but to transmit that news for commercial use, in competition with complainant—which is what defendant has done and seeks to justify—is a very different matter." Even here, however, Pitney saw the need for limits, and suggested that

INS be prohibited from appropriating AP news only "until its commercial value as news to the complainant and all of its members has passed away."

Justice Louis Brandeis dissented. In a lengthy opinion that searched every plausible corner of intellectual property law, he could find no precedent to support the newly innovated misappropriation doctrine. If a new intellectual property doctrine is to encroach on the public domain, he argued, it must come from the democratically elected Congress, not the Presidentially appointed judiciary. And AP's argument about its substantial investment in news gathering did not sway Brandeis. "The fact that a product of the mind has cost its producer money and labor, and has a value for which others are willing to pay, is not sufficient to ensure to it this legal attribute of property. The general rule of law is, that the noblest of human productions—knowledge, truths ascertained, conceptions, and ideas—become, after voluntary communication to others, free as the air to common use."

Intellectual property law's divide between private property and the public domain is a legal artifact, not a natural phenomenon. The line shifts not only with the views of particular judges but also with national boundaries and with cultural attitudes. For many years, United States copyright protection for any work ended after twenty-eight years, and the work then went into the public domain; by contrast, in many European countries copyright does not end until seventy years after the author's death. Some time ago, African nations led a movement to obtain intellectual property protection for indigenous folklore, often hundreds of years old, against appropriation by writers and publishers in industrialized countries. When an American copyright expert challenged an Egyptian folklore advocate—"Surely, folklore is in the public domain"—the Egyptian replied icily, "Public domain is a *very* Western concept."

One reason copyright's metaphysics are so elusive is that its underlying physics are so unstable. Where other American laws may be driven by a single, widely shared purpose, copyright's foundations are split by debate. On one side are lawyers who assert that copyright is rooted in natural justice, entitling authors to every last penny that other people will pay to obtain copies of their works. These are the copyright optimists: they view copyright's cup of entitlement as always half full, only waiting to be filled still further. On the other side of the debate are copyright pessimists, who see copyright's cup as half empty: they accept that copyright owners should get some measure of control over copies as an incentive to produce creative works, but they would like copyright to extend only so far as is necessary to give this incentive, and treat anything more as an encroachment on the general freedom of everyone to write and say what they please.

A law drafted by a copyright optimist to reward the novelist Margaret Mitchell for the popular success of her novel, *Gone with the Wind*, would look very different from a law drafted by a copyright pessimist. The copyright optimist would enact a law entitling Mitchell and her publisher to every corner of the market for the novel's content: hardcover and paperback book sales; film revenue from any movie based on the novel; dramatic renditions, television broadcasts, audio or videocassette sales and rentals; translations of the novel or films into other languages; publication of sequels (one sequel, *Scarlett*, commanded a $4.94 million advance against royalties for Mitchell's estate).

The copyright pessimist would write a law based on the answer to just one question: How much money would it have taken to get Margaret Mitchell to sit down at her desk to write *Gone with the Wind* and to get her publisher to publish it? In a commentary on the 2 Live Crew case, the *New York Times* critic Jon Pareles wrote, "Any song that is well enough known to make a takeoff worthwhile has probably already raked in plenty of profits from sales, licensing agreements, sheet music, etc. Sometimes I'm tempted to suggest that any song that has sold more than a million (or maybe two million or five million) copies ought to go directly into the public domain, as if its fans have ransomed it from the copyright holders." Edward Murphy, president of the National Music Publishers' Association, did not take this tongue-in-cheek suggestion lightly. "This outrageously regressive attitude," he wrote to the editor of the *Times*, "has been rejected by nearly every government in the world." Pressing the point home, he added that copyright protection "serves as the cornerstone of the *Times*'s ability to protect its proprietary intellectual property interests throughout the world."

A singular phenomenon fuels the debate over copyright: copyright encompasses one of the few areas of human effort in which one person can "use" something without diminishing the ability of anyone else to do the same. A loaf of bread, once eaten, is gone. But "Oh, Pretty Woman," once sung and heard, is still available for someone else to sing and to hear. Countless fans can listen to the song, indeed copy it, without diminishing its availability to anyone else who wants to sing or listen to or copy it.

The copyright debate divides on the implications of this phenomenon. Copyright optimists say that since entertainment and information products can be "used" endlessly without being consumed, there is no harm in extending copyright to encompass the economically valuable uses that may fill copyright's cup, always half full, still more. Since a work's author created all this value, he is entitled to reap its full reward. The copyright pessimists view the same phenomenon more skeptically. Make a copy of a friend's computer spreadsheet program; jot down a favorite recipe; videotape a motion picture off the television set—who is harmed? If a copyrighted work can be so easily viewed or copied without causing evident discomfort to anyone, what harm is there in excusing these additional uses from copyright liability—particularly if copyright owners continue to produce new works anyway?

Each side in the battle regularly invokes some larger truth to support its cause—"natural rights" for the optimists, "individual freedoms" for the pessimists. But the resolutions reached by legislators and judges are simply legal conclusions that possess no independent claim on truth. When the federal district court in Nashville ruled that 2 Live Crew was free to record its parody, that became the law and remained so until an appellate court decided differently—which the Sixth Circuit Court of Appeals did in August 1992, ruling that the 2 Live Crew version was too "blatantly commercial" to qualify for the parody defense. The Supreme Court could then change the law again—in March 1993 it agreed to hear the case—as could Congress if it disagreed with the Supreme Court result.

Is copyright protection needed as an incentive to creative production? One reason the copyright optimists resist the pessimists' claim so strongly is that they know that, if put to rigorous empirical proofs, they would often have a hard time answering this vital question affirmatively. The trial court's ruling that 2 Live Crew's parody was unlikely to affect the market for the original song gave Acuff-Rose the virtually impossible task of proving that Orbison and Dees would not have written their song had they known that others could lampoon it for free. The appellate decision, reversing the trial court, simply accepted on faith that the parody would interfere with the market for the Orbison-Dees original and shifted to 2 Live Crew the equally difficult factual burden of proving that Orbison and Dees did not need control over parodies to stimulate their efforts.

Every major clash over copyright, in the United States at any rate, is at bottom a clash between the view that copyright's cup is half full and the view that it is half empty. Sometimes the copyright optimists prevail: the most casual expression—even a quickly scribbled shopping list—automatically gets copyright protection for the full copyright term, although no one needs copyright as an incentive to compile a shopping list. Private letters get copyright protection. (In the case that gave rise to Justice Story's observation, the court ruled that the defendant's biography infringed the copyright in George Washington's letters.) Even conversations get copyright protection. (Ernest Hemingway's widow lost a copyright claim against A. E. Hotchner, Hemingway's biographer, for quoting from remarks the writer had made in conversations with Hotchner, mainly because Hemingway had implicitly consented to the biographer's use of his words.)

At other times, copyright pessimists prevail. Until the beginning of the twentieth century, they wrote the rules on the formal steps that an author had to take to secure copyright for his work: registration and deposit of copies in the Copyright Office and inscription of copyright's equivalent of a "No Trespassing" sign—"Copyright, 1926, Ernest Hemingway"—on every published copy. These requirements, legislators thought, provided a litmus test for proving the author's intention to rely on copyright to protect his work. (Few compilers of shopping lists would trouble to comply with such formalities.) But, beginning in 1909, the copyright optimists succeeded in whittling away these requirements, and today none of them is required to secure copyright. A letter, a conversation, a shopping list has full copyright protection from the moment it is written down, with no need for registration, deposit, notice, or examination in the Copyright Office.

Both sides agree on one crucial point: copyright protects only a work's expression, not its underlying ideas. This rule often comes as an unhappy surprise to the legions of aspiring moguls who each week send off ideas for new television series or movies to television networks and film studios, only to receive letters—if they receive any response at all—telling them that ideas are not copyrightable. So long as the network or studio does not use the precise words in which the submitter couched his idea, it is free to use the idea itself. (Usually the company has already considered and rejected the same idea from some other source.)

One reason copyright optimists do not oppose this distinction between idea and expression is that they know that ideas—even before they are embodied in specific words—are the taproot of all creativity. Few plots, for example, have not already been invented; were one to protect plots with copyright, that would effectively stop almost everyone from writing novels or making movies. Courts have heeded the wise observation of Oliver Wendell Holmes, Sr., a prominent copyright litigant and father of a Supreme Court Justice, that "literature is full of such coincidences, which some love to believe plagiarisms. There are thoughts always abroad in the air, which it takes more wit to avoid than to hit upon."

The rule that one author can legally borrow another's ideas

explains why copyrights are much less fearsome than patents, which do protect ideas. One might think that the publisher of a popular novel could make its readers pay an extortionate price for a copy of it, just as the owner of a patented drug can extract large payments from patients whose lives depend on a daily pill. But no entertainment or information product enjoys so complete a monopoly as a drug does. Since one writer can freely exploit the ideas, themes, or plots originated by another, any publisher foolish enough to charge $75 for a popular novel would see most of the writer's fans flock to his closest imitator at $19.95, or to any one of the classics now in the public domain and priced at $6.95.

Copyright pessimists have succeeded in installing other safety valves. One is the concept of the compulsory license. Under the Copyright Act's very few compulsory license provisions, anyone can, upon paying a statutorily fixed fee, use an author's work without even contacting him. For example, once a song is recorded with the author's consent, anyone else can record his own version of it, provided he pays a prescribed royalty of 6.25 cents for each copy he makes, which may explain why there are so many renditions of popular songs by different artists—"covers," as they are called. In fact, 2 Live Crew sought shelter under this compulsory license provision of the Copyright Act, depositing $13,867.56 for the copies it made of "Oh, Pretty Woman." But the group did not pursue this line of argument—probably because the compulsory license does not encompass travesties or parodies made of an original.

Fair use is another safety valve. The Copyright Act allows the copying of copyrighted material if it is done for a salutary purpose—news reporting, teaching, criticism are examples— and if other statutory factors weigh in its favor. When the reclusive billionaire Howard Hughes tried to suppress the factual sources that his potential biographers might draw on by buying up the copyrights to magazine articles that had been written about him, the court ruled that fair use protected anyone who quoted from the articles. Or, when *Life* magazine, which had acquired the copyright to the amateur photographer Abraham Zapruder's film of the assassination of President John F. Kennedy, sought to enjoin the reproduction of frames from the film in a book about the assassination, the court ruled that the copying was fair use. In the *Pretty Woman* case, 2 Live Crew rested its parody defense on the fair use doctrine.

These and other safety valves have buffered copyright from charges that it violates the First Amendment's guarantees of free speech and press. In 1984, *The Nation* magazine argued to the Supreme Court that the First Amendment entitled it to quote key passages from Gerald Ford's still unpublished memoirs dealing with his pardon of Richard Nixon. The Court answered that First Amendment protections are "already embodied in the Copyright Act's distinction between copyrightable expression and uncopyrightable facts and ideas, and the latitude for scholarship and comment traditionally afforded by fair use." "In our haste to disseminate news," Justice Sandra Day O'Connor wrote, "it should not be forgotten that the Framers intended copyright itself to be the engine of free expression."

The ongoing debate over copyright's proper reach, and the unpredictability with which courts and Congress resolve it, can produce painful surprises. One—it must have been a surprise to Groucho Marx—is that copyright infringement can be a crime. In 1938, the Ninth Circuit Court of Appeals in California affirmed Marx's conviction for broadcasting a comic skit based on a copyrighted script, "The Hollywood Adventures of Mr. Dibble and Mr. Dabble," which its authors had earlier submitted to Marx but for which the comedian had failed to obtain a license. In 1992, hoping to suppress criminal piracy more effectively, Congress boosted criminal copyright infringement from misdemeanor to felony status, with a sanction of up to five years in prison.

While the two sides may disagree on the proper scope of copyright protection, they do agree that some level of protection is needed to spur the production and distribution of creative work that is intended for copying. But what if it could be shown that copyright is in fact *not* needed as an incentive? This was the radical question that a thirty-two-year-old assistant professor at the Harvard Law School undertook in his first major article, "The Uneasy Case for Copyright," published in 1971 in the prestigious *Harvard Law Review*. Stephen Breyer's essay—his "tenure piece" that would win him a permanent post at Harvard—was nothing less than an attempt to dismantle the moral and economic claims that undergirded two hundred years of copyright law in the United States. (Twenty-three years later, after a series of career changes, Breyer became the 108th Justice of the Supreme Court.)

Professor Breyer's article came at a critical moment, for Congress and the courts were just beginning to address a new copyright battleground: whether copyright should encompass copying by such new technologies as the photocopier, home audiotape and videotape machines, and computers. If the article's title left any doubt about its implications for the technological maelstrom that copyright was about to enter, the subtitle dispelled it: "A Study of Copyright in Books, Photocopies, and Computer Programs."

In the first part of his essay Breyer attacked the natural

rights rationale for copyright, so often invoked by copyright optimists. Against the claim that authors should be paid according to the value of their work to society, Breyer observed that "few workers receive salaries that approach the total value of what they produce." Nor, he wrote, is there anything inherently immoral about this, since the difference between the value of a worker's effort and the amount he is paid for it is passed on to the consumer in the form of a lower price for the product. Breyer thus dismissed the "intuitive, unanalyzed feeling" that an author's work is his property. "We do not ordinarily create or modify property rights, nor even award compensation, solely on the basis of labor expended."

Breyer's heart was clearly in the data and analysis that followed, occupying sixty of his article's seventy pages, in which he took on the foundational economic premise of American copyright law: that copyright is needed as an incentive to produce and distribute creative works. Among his economic arguments, two stand out: that, even without copyright, an original publisher can ward off unauthorized copies of a written work by threatening to issue a "fighting edition" priced even lower than the pirate's; and that, although it costs a pirate less to publish a book than it costs the original publisher, the latter has a lead-time advantage that enables it to recoup its costs. Breyer estimated that "by the time a copier chooses a book, prints it, and distributes it to retailers, he may be six to eight weeks behind, by which time the initial publisher will have provided retailers with substantial inventories. It is unlikely that a price difference of less than a dollar will lead many retailers and customers to wait for a cheaper edition, for hardbound book customers do not seem to respond readily to price reductions. They are not willing, after all, to wait for a cheaper paperbound edition."

Breyer's article unsettled the copyright bar. Lawmakers had historically accepted on faith the need for copyright, asking only where to draw the line of liability. Now, with Breyer's manifesto in hand, congressional committees might initiate legislative free-for-alls with uncertain outcomes for copyright. Courts might tip the balance in close cases in favor of copyright defendants. Most unsettling, the logic of Breyer's challenge did not stop at copyright in books. Was copyright also unnecessary in the world of motion pictures, sound recordings, and magazines? Should copyright prohibit the home copying of movies or records? Library photocopying of printed material? For an entire season, one question dominated discussions among copyright lawyers from New York to Los Angeles: How can we respond to Stephen Breyer? Who will respond to him?

The task ultimately fell to Barry Tyerman, a third-year student at UCLA Law School, in an article published in his own school's law review. Breyer's argument that the initial publisher could fend off copiers with the threat of a "fighting edition" offended Tyerman's practical sense of things. "How many times could a publisher sell drastically below his costs to drive out a copier and still remain financially solvent? It is no answer to say that a publisher could subsidize production of these 'fighting editions' from the excess profits earned on his other titles." In Tyerman's view, the book market is easy to enter, and high profits on *any* title would attract competition. "There would be no safe haven in which the initial publisher could produce a book free from competition in that title and make the profits necessary to finance the production and sales of 'fighting editions' of other titles."

Tyerman also had to answer Breyer's argument that in a

world without copyright, even though it might cost a competitor less to make copies of a book than it did the initial publisher, the latter has a lead-time advantage that enables it to recoup its production costs. Tyerman's response was again simple and factual: Why should we assume that the copier's unauthorized edition would be a paperback edition rather than a more expensive hardcover one? And, in any event, the competing, illicit copy would reach the market sooner than an authorized cheaper edition, which publishers intentionally delay. "The alleged price insensitivity of book *consumers* may be largely irrelevant since to a great degree it is book *distributors* (who as a group tend to be much more price conscious), and not the public, who actually determine the character of the retail market for most books."

Breyer's analysis was open to another criticism. In focusing on the quantity of books that would be produced without copyright, he had ignored the effect that the elimination of copyright would have on the quality of books. Publishers would, if they could, have all the works they issue enjoy great commercial success. But because they cannot be completely prescient, they spread their investment among a number of works, hoping that higher sales on some will compensate for low sales on others. In a world without copyright, copiers would enjoy a signal advantage: they could choose to copy only those works that sell well, thus cutting into the authorized publisher's ability to compensate for less successful titles with income from those that sell better.

The debate ended with a brief rejoinder from Breyer in which he quickly backpedaled away from his original, bold inquiry: "The important debate, as Mr. Tyerman surely recognizes, is not whether copyright should be abolished, but whether, and how, copyright's strictures should be modified." Breyer had evidently departed from the radical camp and joined the copyright pessimists.

Breyer's thesis, and the response to it, would have struck copyright lawyers in most countries outside the United States as bizarre. European, Asian, and Latin American nations have copyright laws that look and work in many respects like American copyright law. But, unlike copyright law in the United States, Britain, and countries of the former British Empire, their copyright laws rest squarely on the natural rights philosophy that Breyer dismissed as the "intuitive, un-analyzed feeling" that an author's work is his property. To these countries, an author's work is not only his property but the very embodiment of his personality. So firmly do these countries believe that an author is morally entitled to control the product of his labors that lawmakers will not even entertain the debate between America's copyright optimists and pessimists.

The differences in premises and operational details that separate American copyright law from copyright in most of the rest of the world sometimes complicate the efforts of American copyright owners to sell their works abroad. For copyright is also territorial. If an American work is copied in Germany, German, not American, law determines whether the copying has infringed copyright, and whether the copyright holder is entitled to compensation. Because German copyright law differs from American copyright law, American copyright holders may be able to control uses of their works in Germany that they could not control in the United States, and vice versa.

Nations around the world have tried to smooth over the rough edges of different legal systems through multilateral treaty arrangements. But these copyright treaties offer no help to foreign authors in countries that either have not signed a copyright treaty or refuse to enforce their treaty obligations. Since 1986, more than 50 million copies of translated Agatha Christie mysteries have reportedly been sold in Russia, for example, most without any royalties being paid to the author's estate or to her publisher. When the Khudozhestvennaya Literatura, a Russian publishing house, paid a large advance to Margaret Mitchell's estate for the Russian-language rights to *Scarlett*, the authorized sequel to *Gone with the Wind*, it evidently did not anticipate copycats springing up in St. Petersburg, Khabarovsk, and Novosibirsk; but they did.

The patchwork quilt of international copyright has complicated copyright practice for more than a century, and the cascading explosion of new information and entertainment technologies will produce even greater dislocations. Technologies for digitally storing and transmitting works will radically alter some markets, while others will remain untouched. (And although savants have regularly predicted the death of the book, the future will probably continue to prove them wrong; over the past forty years, the number of bookstores and books published has quadrupled.) Will copyright, which has for so long mediated between authors and audiences, be up to the challenges posed by the new information and entertainment environment?

Copyright was technology's child from the start. There was no need for copyright before the printing press. But as movable type brought literature within the reach of everyone, and as the preferences of a few royal, aristocratic, or simply wealthy patrons were supplanted by the accumulated demands of mass consumers, a legal mechanism was needed to connect consumers to authors and publishers commercially.

Copyright was the answer. Centuries later, photographs, sound recordings, motion pictures, videocassette recorders, compact discs, and digital computers have dramatically expanded the markets for mechanically reproduced entertainment and information, and increased copyright's function in ordering these markets.

The future promises dazzling new possibilities for access to entertainment and information: a celestial jukebox. Whether it takes the form of a technology-packed satellite orbiting thousands of miles above the earth or remains entirely earthbound, linked by cable, fiber optics, and telephone wires, the celestial jukebox will give millions of people access to a vast range of films, sound recordings, and printed material, awaiting only a subscriber's electronic command for it to pop up on his television or computer screen. It is 2 a.m. and a subscriber in Idaho wants to see the film *Cape Fear*. Which version does he prefer: the 1962 production starring Robert Mitchum, Gregory Peck, and Polly Bergen, or the 1991 version with Robert De Niro, Nick Nolte, and Jessica Lange? Moments after he enters his selection of one or the other, the film's sounds and images will surface on his video monitor with sparkling, lifelike clarity.

None of this will come free. The celestial jukebox will bill subscribers much as the telephone company does or, if it is linked to the subscriber's bank account, by simply debiting his balance. Pricing may be more refined, however. Where the telephone company charges calls on the basis of length and time of day, the celestial jukebox will also be able to charge according to the value of the work transmitted. It may price the 1962 version of *Cape Fear* at two dollars, and the 1991 version at five, depending on demand. The bookkeeping will be automatic. Before signing off with a comforting beep, the system will execute one last command, billing the subscriber's account.

The celestial jukebox will contain computer software that can in a moment scan hundreds of databases to pick out the latest items of interest to the subscribers' business or hobby. Lawyers have for years been able to retrieve the latest judicial decision or statutory enactment by simply pressing a few buttons on a computer keyboard. If a subscriber wants daily reports on athletic events, software will instantaneously scout and assemble these items for him, delivering a custom-tailored sports newsletter to his doorstep or computer mailbox. Software-driven databases can help the subscriber with his shopping—or his child with a school science project—enabling each to start with the most general description of his interests and then to focus in as he wishes on more and more specific information.

Over the past twenty-five years, new devices such as high-speed photocopiers and inexpensive home audiotape and videotape machines have threatened to undercut copyright's ability to return a work's value to its producer. Free photocopies of articles from scholarly journals borrowed from libraries displace subscriptions to the journals themselves; home audiotapes and videotapes of broadcast sound recordings and films mean one less trip to the record store, video rental store, or motion picture theater. These shifts might appear to suggest that copyright should be extended to encompass these new uses. But, reluctant to extend copyright into the privacy of the home, Congress and the courts have declined to treat these uses as copyright infringements.

For copyright optimists, at least, one virtue of the celestial jukebox is that it can reverse the losses they see copyright owners suffering today when people make copies of films and sound recordings: by charging subscribers electronically for each use of the prerecorded works it offers—motion pictures, sound recordings, books, magazines or newspaper articles— the celestial jukebox will be able to compensate copyright owners each time their works are chosen. With the audience increasing and distribution costs decreasing, the price of access to these works should drop sharply to well below the prices now paid, so that people would simply not bother making copies off the air, knowing they can obtain any work on the celestial jukebox any time they want.

If Congress and the courts continue to hesitate to extend copyright into the home, and copyright law's public-private distinction persists and is not adjusted to the technologies of the celestial jukebox, the integrity of copyright will be threatened. Any parent who has ever hosted a child's birthday party will probably be shocked to learn that the song "Happy Birthday" is protected by a copyright that will not expire until the year 2010, though relieved to learn that copyright prohibits only *public* performances of the song, so that if a party takes place at home, among "a normal circle of a family and social acquaintances," no copyright infringement now occurs. But performances enjoyed by means of celestial jukebox will also occur in the privacy of the home. Will Congress say that these performances, if unauthorized, infringe copyright? If not, copyright owners stand to lose a great part of their products' value.

New digital technologies are already challenging copyright. Digital sampling technology—which, by converting sounds to digital computer code, can break them into fragments as small as a single musical note—could take Paul McCartney's voice from an early Beatles recording and, with no effort on his part, have him singing an aria from *Rigoletto*.

(One of Acuff-Rose's experts testified at trial that 2 Live Crew may have digitally sampled a portion of Orbison's recording of "Oh, Pretty Woman.") Animated images of Humphrey Bogart, Jimmy Cagney, and Groucho Marx snatched from old black-and-white films can be colorized and seamlessly injected into filmed advertisements featuring their video counterparts fifty years later. Where do a copyright owner's rights begin and end in this atomized, ever-changing environment?

The computer's ability to break a work down into digital fragments and to recombine these fragments with bits and pieces from other works and databases means that an author who commits his work to a digital database exposes it irretrievably to a potentially indeterminate degree of sampling, rearrangement, and recombination. Motion picture directors today complain when studios colorize their black-and-white films, when broadcasters "pan and scan" to squeeze their filmed images into the changed spatial proportions of the home television screen, or edit or compress them to fit into broadcast television's predetermined time slots. What will happen when digital sampling shreds their works into bits and pieces, free for users to recombine into entirely different forms?

On more distant frontiers, computer programs may one day displace living authors in creating certain kinds of products that inform and entertain. Today's computer-generated weather maps may someday be joined by even more elaborate products of artificial intelligence, all produced at the mere cost of the electricity that it takes to run the computer. Like so many other products of the digital environment, computer-created works challenge traditional copyright assumptions. At a recent international conference convoked in

California's Silicon Valley to address the copyright questions raised by artificial intelligence, the director general of the World Intellectual Property Organization persistently asked, "Who is the *author* of what *work*?"

Book publishers and music publishers, motion picture and record producers are understandably wary about copyright's ability to secure their investments in this new digital environment. They are only beginning to assess the risks of depositing—or failing to deposit—the products they sell in digital storehouses. Putting their products on line promises new revenues. But will the new revenues be equal to the revenues they displace? And will committing the products to a digital environment put them outside copyright control? Yet keeping the products off line risks ceding to their competitors the only market that matters.

The power that a celestial jukebox would give copyright owners to separate paying from nonpaying audiences may seem a happy boon to copyright optimists. But it could also become society's nightmare. The public today gets most of its daily information and entertainment "free," or at least for far less than it costs, over commercial television and radio and in newspapers and magazines, because these media get revenue from commercial advertising. With the celestial jukebox, while the quantity of entertainment and information will doubtless increase for those who are able and willing to pay for it, it will probably shrink for those who are not. Will advertisers want to go on paying for air time, or for newspaper and magazine space, that will reach only poorer—and shrinking—audiences?

As the pace of technological change quickens, Congress seems less and less able to adjust copyright laws to the changes. In the two centuries since it passed the first American copyright act, it has been playing catch-up with new technologies—first photographs, then phonograph records, motion pictures, radio, broadcast television, and cable television—usually about twenty years behind the new technologies. As new copying technologies—audiotape and videotape machines, personal computers—spread through America today, the idea of subjecting them to copyright control has become politically unpalatable. Observing what he called the "iron law of consensus," a former staff member of a Senate copyright subcommittee has cautioned not to look to Congress for help if any proposed imposition of copyright liability disrupts entrenched consumer habits. Ten years ago, at a symposium on copyright and the new technologies, organized by the Copyright Office and the chairmen of the relevant House and Senate subcommittees, one speaker remarked, "When you are working on the cutting edge of technology, the main thing is to stay behind the blade," a view that the chairman of the House intellectual property subcommittee embraced a year later.

Copyright owners have regularly expected the federal courts, particularly the Supreme Court, to protect them against the threats posed by new technologies. If Congress takes twenty years to bring a new technological use under copyright control, perhaps the Supreme Court could be convinced more quickly to interpret the existing copyright laws as encompassing the new use. But with few exceptions—most notably, opinions written by Justice Oliver Wendell Holmes, Jr., decades ago—the Court's attitude has been to treat copyright's cup as half empty, not half full.

Many Supreme Court watchers were surprised when the

Court agreed to hear the *Pretty Woman* appeal. It rarely takes more than one copyright appeal a year, and the dispute between Acuff-Rose and 2 Live Crew appeared to present none of the legal issues the Court usually chooses to address. But evidently the Justices saw some larger issue lurking between the tracks of "Me So Horny" and "My Seven Bizzos."

The Supreme Court handed down its unanimous decision in March 1994, reversing the Court of Appeals ruling for Acuff-Rose. Writing for the Court, Justice David Souter categorically rejected the notion that the commercial success of the 2 Live Crew album foreclosed a fair use defense. Commercialism is copyright's credo, after all; the traditional contexts of fair use—news reporting, comment, criticism—are all commonly pursued for profit. More important, parody is a "transformative use," altering the original to create a new work. "The goal of copyright, to promote science and the arts, is generally furthered by the creation of transformative works." At bottom, Souter sought to align copyright principle with good artistic practice. As the eighteenth-century composer and musical theorist Johann Mattheson once observed about melodic invention: "Borrowing is a permissible action; one must however return what is borrowed with interest, that is, one must arrange and work out the imitation that it has a better and more beautiful appearance than the object from which it has been borrowed."

The world that copyright touches has changed dramatically since Justice Story speculated on the law's metaphysics in a case involving George Washington's letters a century and a half ago. Copycats who did little more than duplicate an entire book verbatim have been joined by more creative copiers—authors in their own right—who impose their creative efforts on the works of others, translating novels from English into Russian, transforming stories into motion pictures, recording parodies of popular songs, sampling elements from digital databases. The technology of the printing press has been joined by fabulous new machines for copying, storing, and manipulating words, images, and sounds—machines that can make everyman his own author or director, publisher or film producer.

But the puzzle of copyright's metaphysics remains unchanged: where should copyright draw the line between the competing works of creative minds? Copyright's constantly careening physics also remain intractable: should legislatures and courts treat copyright's cup as half full or as half empty?

Copyright moves purposefully through these domestic and global crosscurrents, buffeted sometimes, but also exerting the steadying force of almost three centuries' history in ordering markets for information and entertainment. Other more familiar bodies of law—contracts, torts, and crimes—have an even longer history, but none occupies this special place in ordering a nation's culture, high and low, and in helping to preserve authorial autonomy. Copyright is unique. In connecting supply to demand, creators to consumers, authors to their audiences, copyright gives producers the legal implements they need to offer their work to customers.

This book is about copyright; about the world of information and entertainment it sustains; the new technologies that, along with the old and in harness with the creative spirit, promise to alter this environment dramatically; and about the decisions that will have to be made in the United States and around the world if the new environment is to flourish. This book does not ask, as would some legal specialists, whether copyright will survive the new technologies. That question is about as bootless as asking whether politics will survive democracy. The real question is what steps it will take to ensure that the promised new era of information and entertainment survives copyright.

History offers a clue.

CHAPTER TWO

The History of an Idea

Every encounter between copyright and a new technology, from the printing press to the celestial jukebox, has presented a stark choice for lawmakers: to expand copyright so that authors and publishers can capture the work's value in the marketplace; or to withhold copyright, in which case people can enjoy copies of the work free. Is copyright an author's right, giving the originator a claim on every market in which consumers will pay for copies? Or is it a user's right, entitling the user to enjoy a copy free unless the author and his publisher can show that, if they are not paid, they will have no incentive to create and publish new works?

Close to three centuries of legislation, court decisions, and scholarly reflection have left these fundamental questions unresolved. The U.S. Congress sometimes greets the invention of a new information technology as an occasion to fill up the cup of copyright with yet another legal right. Other times, it declines to bring a new market within the law's embrace. Judges are similarly ambivalent. When Congress leaves its intentions unclear, some judges will read the Copyright Act expansively to cover a new technology; others stick strictly to the words of the old statute. Law professors also take sides, some joining the "high protectionists," others the "low protectionists." (These are perjoratives, not merit badges; academics pin these labels on their adversaries, never themselves.)

Copyright touches directly on conflicting cultural, economic, and political values—the desire for art and literature; a commitment to free markets; traditions of free speech. The debate over the course of the law has attracted more than its share of literary thinkers: John Milton in the *Areopagitica*, excoriating government censorship but supporting copyright; Edmund Burke and Oliver Goldsmith finding time to attend the arguments before the House of Lords in the first great case to test the reach of copyright; John Hersey entering an impassioned dissent from a U.S. government commission report proposing to bring computer programs within copyright. Copyright's conflicts have also inspired great judges to some of their deepest observations—Lord Mansfield staking out the argument for a robust copyright; Oliver Wendell Holmes writing a brilliant series of opinions that transformed a fusty and rigid nineteenth-century copyright into an open, pliant doctrine that could accommodate the tensions of twentieth-century technologies.

The historical antiphonies have a deep past. Behind the expansionist case for copyright is the ethical sense that it is unjust to deprive authors of the reward for their labors, to allow second comers to reap where they have not sown. But the low protectionists, too, make a claim on justice. Why, they ask, should writers get more money than they need to get them to the writing table? Anything more than this is a windfall better shared in the form of lower prices for their readers.

And, they add, every writer invariably draws on the works and traditions of earlier writers; since they all borrow from others, they should share some part of their revenue with succeeding generations.

The moral impulse to protect authors is much older than copyright. The Roman poet Martial inveighed against the unauthorized recitation of his works as *plagium*—kidnapping—leaving no doubt about his idea of the bond that ties an author to his work. (Though courts even today will sometimes characterize copyright infringement as plagiarism, more precisely the term means what Martial meant—a writer's false claim that another's work is his own.) According to legend, when the sixth-century monk Columba secretly copied a psalter belonging to the Abbot Finian, King Diarmid ordered the unauthorized copy given to the Abbot: "To every cow her calf, and to every book its copy."

Until the printing press, few occasions arose to assert these moral claims. A pirate who copied an author's manuscript by hand had to invest the same physical labor as the author or scribe who penned the original; the cost advantage of the pirated copy was virtually nil. But the printing press, and later improvements in printing technology, dramatically altered the economics of authorship. Cheaper copies meant larger audiences, and larger audiences brought the prospect of greater revenues overall. As the cost of printing declined, the relative value of each copy's literary content increased. For the first time, the value of the author's genius could outweigh the cost of the scrivener's labor. The arithmetic is straightforward: simply subtract the manufacturing and distribution cost of a copy from the price the public will pay for it; what remains is the value of the author's contribution.

The printing press irrevocably altered the balance of moral and economic claims to works of authorship. It also presented copyright law's central question: Who should be entitled to share in the newly opened cache of literary value? The author who created the text? The publisher who financed the risk that copies of the text might never find enough readers to re-pay the cost of printing and distributing it? Or—once author and publisher were paid—the public, in the form of lower prices? And what of the genius whose mechanical invention, the printing press, first liberated this value? (Beginning in the late sixteenth century, royal patents for mechanical devices such as printing presses effectively gave inventors the oppor-tunity to share in the value that their inventions created.)

For close to two centuries in England, these competing en-titlements were allocated strictly by the Crown for both po-litical and economic reasons. The uncontrolled dissemination of literary works and political treatises could invite sedition; also, printing, along with other emerging industries, gave the Crown a new source of revenue and favors. By granting an exclusive right—a patent, it was called—to print particular literary or legal or educational works to a given bookseller, the English sovereigns were able to tap into a continuing stream of loyalty and income.

However important they may have been to their owners, the printing patents were of small economic consequence. Doubtless, their inconsequentiality helped insulate them from the massive parliamentary and judicial attack on other Crown patents, such as those on salt, starch, and vinegar, in the late sixteenth and the early seventeenth centuries. (Patents for technological inventions also survived the onslaught; they were the precursor of modern patent law.) Another reason the printing patents endured was because of a shrewd alliance between the Crown and the Stationers' Company, which prolonged the printing monopoly for close to another hundred years.

Well before printing arrived in England, the Stationers' Company had set up business in London as a guild of scribes, bookbinders, and booksellers. Over the years, it became a closely knit, powerful cartel with a single object—maintaining order and profits in the publishing trade. By the mid-sixteenth century, printers replaced scribes on the Company's rolls, and the Company itself replaced the Crown as the immediate source of the authority to print, bind, and sell books. Subject only to the Crown's ultimate authority, the Stationers' power over the publishing trade in England was absolute. No member of the Company—and, by design, virtually every English printer was a member—could publish a work without the Company's consent. The Company had the power to search out, seize, and destroy offending works.

The Stationers' rights were perpetual, passing from one generation of printers to the next. Writers had no place in the Company. A Stationer would, typically, purchase from the author for a lump sum the right to print and distribute a text; the only property right the author had in his work was in the physical manuscript, the paper and ink in which he had expressed himself. He had no right to exploit the value of the texts themselves. Since only a Stationer was allowed to print a book, the author's sole rights were in the terms that controlled the text's first publication. When John Milton assented to the publication of *Paradise Lost,* he undertook to "give, grant, and assigne, unto the said Sam. Symons, his executors and assignes, All that Booke, Copy or Manuscript of a Poem intituled Paradise lost . . . now lately Licensed to be printed . . ."

. . . now lately Licensed to be printed. Here was the key to the Crown's continuing control over political dissent. The printers enjoyed and enforced a monopoly over publishing. But, under the Licensing Act and successive edicts, orders, and decrees, the printers could publish only books licensed by the Crown. Under these laws, the Crown determined what works could be published; under the printing patent, the Stationers suppressed trade not only in unauthorized copies of licensed works, but in unlicensed works as well. The Stationers got the economic rewards of monopoly; in return, the Crown got from the Stationers a ruthlessly efficient enforcer of the censorship. When Milton wrote the *Areopagitica*—one of the rare works published without Crown license or registration with the Stationers' Company—he drew a sharp line between the Crown's political agenda and the Company's commercial aims, attacking the censorship but acknowledging the propriety of that part of the ordinance that ensured "the just retaining of each man his several copies (which God forbid should be gainsaid)."

The Licensing Act expired in 1694, and with it the principal sanction behind the Stationers' monopoly. (From 1695 on, the Crown sought to control dissent through criminal prosecutions for seditious libel.) Although the Company retained nominal control over the printing trade, it had lost its most potent weapon—the power to seize, destroy, and levy fines against offending works and presses. The only sanction left to the publishers was an action for monetary damages in the law courts. And there, they complained, it was impossible for a publisher "to prove the tenth or hundredth part of damages he suffers, because 1000 counterfeit copies may be dispersed into as many different hands, all over the kingdom, and he is not able to prove the sale of 10."

After years of failed efforts to extend their censorship, the Stationers shifted their legislative strategy. In place of their own lost profits, they now put the interests of writers and readers at the fore. Beginning in 1706, the Stationers petitioned Parliament that authors would not write new works without the security of an easily enforced property right. Out of three years of intense lobbying came the world's first copyright act, the Statute of Anne, "An Act for the Encouragement of Learning, by vesting the Copies of Printed Books in the Authors or Purchasers of such Copies, during the Times therein mentioned." The Statute dramatically changed the allocation of entitlements among authors, publishers, and readers. Severing the enforcement of literary property rights from the Stationers' monopoly, the Statute unleashed a free market for literature and for ideas.

The Statute of Anne confirmed the Stationers' copyrights and gave them the coercive remedies they sought. In return, it redistributed some of the publishers' earlier perquisites to the public and to authors. In place of the formerly perpetual monopoly, the term of copyright protection now ended twenty-eight years after a work's publication; after twenty-eight years, anyone could copy the work and, presumably, sell it to the public. Parliament also split the twenty-eight-year copyright into two fourteen-year terms, so that, even in cases where the author had assigned full copyright in a given work to a publisher, the law returned the copyright to the author at the end of its initial fourteen-year term to enjoy for the second fourteen-year term. The Statute's great revolution was to separate copyright from membership in the Stationers' Company. Anyone in the realm, writers as well as publishers, could get copyright in a work simply by enrolling it on the Company's register.

Parliament made one stinting concession to the Stationers' plea to keep a perpetual monopoly in the works to which they held copyright, giving them a one-time-only twenty-one-year copyright in works that had first been published before the Statute was passed. In the late 1720s, as the end of protection for these books approached, the booksellers once again petitioned Parliament, seeking a return to the comforts of perpetual monopoly. Rebuffed by Parliament, they turned to the English courts, mounting an ingenious legal argument that would frame the terms of copyright debate in England, and later in the United States, right down to the present.

In court, as before in Parliament, the Stationers pitched their argument on the moral claims of authors—claims, they argued, that could not be cabined by the Statute's limited term of protection. The common law of England gave farmers perpetual rights in their real property on the theory that they had mixed their labor with the soil. Why, the Stationers contended, shouldn't the common law also give a perpetual right to authors, whose labor is mixed forever in the texts that embody their ideas? When an author sells a manuscript to a publisher, he is selling not just the tangible manuscript but also a separate and perpetual right to publish the manuscript's contents—a morally compelled natural right with a life entirely apart from the Statute of Anne.

The publishers had more than a theory. They also had a strategy. The strategy was for one of them to bring an action claiming infringement of the common law copyright in Chancery, the arm of the English judiciary empowered to grant injunctions. The publisher would claim that it owned the common law copyright in a work through a transfer from the author, and would allege that the defendant's unauthorized copies of it infringed this right, entirely apart from the

Statute of Anne. If this strategy succeeded, Chancery would temporarily enjoin the defendant pending determination of the facts and governing law. If the Chancery judge had any doubt as to the applicable law—and he surely would, for the Stationers' argument was innovative at best—he would refer the case to the common law courts.

At first, interim relief from Chancery was all the London publishers needed. Temporarily enjoined from printing unauthorized editions, and lacking the resources to pursue the case in the common law courts, the unauthorized printers backed off. But the publishers knew it was only a matter of time before a resourceful printer would pursue the issue in the law courts, where the fate of the claimed perpetual right was far from certain. An appeal to the House of Lords would then be all but inevitable. But from the Stationers' point of view, the House of Lords had to be avoided at all costs. The Lords had consistently resisted their legislative efforts to extend the term of protection under the Statute of Anne, and the Stationers had no reason to expect a warmer judicial reception for their new claim of a perpetual right.

To forestall the possibility of an appeal to the House of Lords, the Stationers struck on the risky tactic of a collusive lawsuit. One of them, a bookseller named Tonson, would sue an unauthorized but obliging printer, Collins, before a judge, Lord Mansfield, whose sympathies to the case for perpetual copyright were well known from his earlier representation of the booksellers. Counsel for the opposing sides, both paid by the booksellers, would argue for and against the existence of the perpetual common law right, Collins's counsel perhaps somewhat less vigorously than Tonson's. Judgment would go against the pirate, who, by prearrangement, would choose not to appeal to the House of Lords. As a result, *Tonson v. Collins,* the lower court decision establishing the perpetual right, would stand as the law of England.

Only one detail foiled this charade. After two successive arguments by counsel, Lord Mansfield ordered the case to be put over for argument before the full court. Then, before the case could be reargued, the judges learned—one wonders how—that the suit was collusive, and they dismissed the action.

A decade later, the London Stationers obtained in *Millar v. Taylor* the judgment they had sought in *Tonson v. Collins*. The work in issue was *The Seasons*, a popular epic poem by James Thomson, who had in 1729 sold the copyright to Andrew Millar, a London bookseller. By 1767, the statutory copyright in the poem had expired, and Robert Taylor, a bookseller outside the Stationers' Company, issued a cheap rival edition. Millar sued, claiming infringement of the purportedly perpetual common law right that Thomson had sold him. The questions before the Court of King's Bench went to the very heart of copyright: Should society give authors an exclusive right to their works? If so, should the author's right be perpetual, or should it last just long enough to give him sufficient revenues to induce continued literary efforts, and allow the public to enjoy unlimited editions of his work once the copyright term had ended?

The Justices of King's Bench were no strangers to the claim of perpetual copyright. As a barrister, Lord Mansfield had been counsel to the London booksellers in two of their early Chancery cases; he was also Chief Justice in *Tonson v. Collins*. A strong debater and brilliant legal mind, Mansfield was the most intimidating presence on King's Bench; in his twelve years on the court, no justice had dared dissent from his views. Perhaps equally talented but less flamboyant, Justice

Joseph Yates had as a barrister represented Collins, the alleged pirate, in the second *Tonson v. Collins* argument before Lord Mansfield.

Since he was Chief Justice, Mansfield delivered his opinion last. To no one's surprise, he agreed with his side justices, Aston and Willes, that a perpetual copyright existed at common law and that the Statute of Anne had neither displaced the right nor limited its term. Mansfield rested his opinion on the theory of natural rights that underlay both real and personal property. "It is *just* that an author should reap the pecuniary profits of his own ingenuity and labor. It is *just* that another should not use his name without his consent. It is *fit* that he should judge when to publish, or whether he even will publish. It is *fit* he should not only choose the time but the manner of publication, how many, what volume, what print. It is *fit* he should choose to whose care he will trust the accuracy and correctness of the impression, in whose honesty he will confide not to foist in additions with other reasoning of the same effect." For Mansfield, the rationale for a property right in unpublished written works applied with equal force to published works such as *The Seasons*; he abruptly dismissed the argument that the Statute of Anne had supplanted the common law.

Justice Yates dissented—the first dissent ever from Chief Justice Mansfield's views—taking three hours to elaborate his position. Yates centered on the claim that ownership can attach to something so fugitive, so entirely outside the claimant's physical possession, as a literary work—an expression, a sentiment—that, once turned loose, is available to all. Common law rights may be secured by possession of a parcel of land or pages of manuscript. But, since the thoughts expressed in the manuscript have no physical dimension, they cannot be possessed, nor can they secure common law rights. A writer can choose not to publish his work. But once published, the work becomes as free as air. "Can he complain of losing the bird he has himself voluntarily turned out?" Why should authors have any greater rights in their thoughts than inventors have in their inventions? Everyone would concede, said Yates, that inventions such as the printing press are not protected outside the scope of the patent statute.

Yates did not dispute the essential merit of Millar's entitlement. "The labours of an author have certainly a right to a reward; but it does not from thence follow, that his reward is to be infinite, and never to have an end." Parliament had passed a law determining the extent of the author's property, and the author had little cause to complain of injustice "after he has enjoyed a monopoly for twenty-eight years, and the manuscript still remains his own property." Yates then upended Mansfield's natural rights argument. Would not a perpetual right for writers encroach on the natural rights of the public? "It is every man's natural right, to follow a lawful employment for the support of himself and his family. Printing and bookselling are lawful employments. And therefore every monopoly that would intrench upon these lawful employments is a strain upon the liberty of the subject."

In 1770, Chancery followed the King's Bench decision for Millar and enjoined Taylor's copies. Taylor filed an appeal to the House of Lords, but the booksellers promptly settled with him to end the case. Millar had not lived to see his ultimate victory, and in 1769 his estate had sold his newly established perpetual right in *The Seasons* to a group of printers; in turn, they were soon forced to undertake a battle of their own.

Alexander Donaldson, a prosperous Scottish bookseller, had already twice been sued by the English booksellers. Now, undeterred by the decisions of King's Bench and Chancery, with an eye to an authoritative decision from the House of Lords and with the resources to obtain it, Donaldson published an unauthorized edition of *The Seasons*. Thomas Becket, *The Seasons'* authorized publisher, went to Chancery for relief; since *Millar v. Taylor* had already established the perpetual common law right, Lord Chancellor Bathurst granted an injunction. Donaldson appealed to the House of Lords. Here at last was the forum that the booksellers had feared, the prospect that had shaped their litigation strategy from the beginning. The House of Lords heard argument in *Donaldson v. Becket* for three weeks, beginning on February 4, 1774, proceedings that attracted tremendous interest. The February 5 issue of the *Morning Chronicle* reported that the "House below the bar . . . was exceedingly crowded," and that "Mr. Edmund Burke, Dr. Goldsmith, David Garrick Esq.; and other literary figures were among the hearers."

Although the Lords' decision in *Donaldson v. Becket* was to be their own, it was customary for them in taking judicial appeals to request advisory opinions from the twelve leading common law judges. The Lords posed five questions to the judges, one of which was central: If England's common law gave authors an exclusive right in their literary works, and if they did not lose this right on publication, did the Statute of Anne abolish that right and limit authors to the Statute's remedies, conditions, and term?

The judges divided on the question, six stating that the statute preempted the common law, five that it did not. Lord Mansfield, who presumably would have tied the vote, declined to give an opinion, "it being very unusual (from reasons of delicacy) for a peer to support his own judgment, upon an appeal to the House of Lords." The reporter of decisions may have miscounted the judges' vote, for there is some evidence that the justices had in fact voted six to five, or even seven to four, that common law copyright survived the Statute of Anne. In any event, the vote was only advisory. It was ultimately the vote of the House of Lords, 22–11 in Donaldson's favor, Lord Mansfield abstaining once again, that became the decision in the case, overturning the Chancery injunction.

Within a week of the Lords' decision, the publishers were back in Parliament seeking relief. Now that the question of perpetual copyright had been definitively decided against them, the publishers presented a more desperate claim. Publishers, they argued, had paid great sums for copyrights to authors and other booksellers on the assumption that the copyrights conveyed would run in perpetuity. With their rights now limited to twenty-eight years, they had lost the benefit of their bargain. A bill favoring the publishers passed the House of Commons but failed in the House of Lords. Lord Mansfield did not attend.

The final outcome of the Stationers' maneuverings would doubtless have pleased Joseph Yates, who resigned from King's Bench less than a year after *Millar v. Taylor* to accept appointment to a lower court and died a few months later. He might have been pleased, too, by Justice Mansfield's last observations on copyright, indicating that the great advocate of natural rights had come around to the view that copyright in fact entails a delicate balance between private and public interests. "We must take care," Lord Mansfield wrote, "to guard against two extremes equally prejudicial; the one, that men of ability, who have employed their time for the service of the community, may not be deprived of their just merits, and the reward of their ingenuity and labour; the other, that the world may not be deprived of improvements, nor the progress of the arts be retarded."

The early years of copyright in the United States paralleled the development of copyright in England in two respects: a copyright act modeled after the Statute of Anne, and a high court case addressing the question whether a natural, common law right survived it. But distinctive forces shaped American copyright law. Writers, not booksellers, led the drive for copyright in the United States. And while colonial printing presses were subject to Crown licensing, no institution in the colonies even approached the Stationers' monopoly over the book trade. Finally, it was a conflict between national and local power, not one between London monopolists and provincial pirates, that dominated the early controversy over copyright in the United States.

Noah Webster, a young schoolmaster, was the most vocal campaigner for copyright in the state legislatures. Fearing that pirated editions would siphon off profits from his *Grammatical Institute of the English Language*, a text that would eventually sell more than 70 million copies, Webster petitioned the state legislatures, one by one, to give him copyright in his book, either through a general copyright statute that, like the Statute of Anne, would encompass the works of all writers in America, or at least through a specific law that would bestow copyright on the *Grammatical Institute*. Other copyright advocates, among them Thomas Paine and Webster's Yale classmate Joel Barlow, lobbied for a general act. Connecticut passed the first statute in 1783, an act "for the Encouragement of Literature and Genius." By 1786, twelve of the thirteen states—Delaware was the single holdout—had enacted copyright statutes, all in the form of a comprehensive, general act.

As the Constitutional Convention drew near, it became

clear to many, including James Madison, that the national interest required a national copyright. Lamenting the Confederation's "want of concert in matters where common interest requires it," Madison noted as an instance "of inferior moment" the lack of uniformity in the laws concerning literary property. The Convention didn't have to revisit the question of the need for copyright, for many of the delegates, George Washington among them, had been present at the debates over the state copyright acts.

On September 5, 1787, less than two weeks before the Constitutional Convention ended, David Brearly of New Jersey presented the proposal of the Committee of Detail for a clause in the Constitution empowering Congress to enact a national copyright law. The clause, which passed unanimously and evidently without debate, linked copyrights to patents: "The Congress shall have Power . . . to promote the Progress of Science and useful Arts, by securing for limited Times to Authors and Inventors the exclusive Right to their respective Writings and Discoveries." (Under usage of the time, "Science" was the subject matter of copyright, "useful Arts" the subject matter of patents.) On May 17, 1790, Congress, exercising the power granted it in this constitutional phrase, passed "An act for the encouragement of learning" that reflected the very practical concerns of a new republic whose geography must have seemed unlimited. The Act gave a fourteen-year copyright not only to "books" but also to maps and charts. President Washington signed the bill into law on May 31, 1790.

That the Constitution empowered Congress to grant copyright for only "limited Times" might appear to have mooted the great question, whether authors have a perpetual right at common law, that had earlier confronted the English courts.

But the constitutional clause constrained only Congress, not the states, and it is the states, not the federal, national government, that are the repositories of common law in the United States. Thus, when a lawsuit first arose questioning whether a common law copyright survived the federal statute, the battle was between state powers and those of the federal government. The case was *Wheaton v. Peters*.

Henry Wheaton was the third Reporter of Decisions of the Supreme Court of the United States; Richard Peters was the fourth. It was the job of the Reporter of Decisions, appointed by the Court, to record, index, abstract, and comment upon the Court's opinions and to arrange for their publication. Wheaton spent twelve exhausting, financially unrewarding years improving the accuracy and timeliness of the Court's reports, all the time embroidering the reports with his own scholarly annotations. He finally resigned and, failing in his efforts to obtain a judicial appointment, accepted a diplomatic post in Denmark. (Foreign service paid better than reporting Supreme Court decisions. As Reporter, Wheaton never earned more than $1,800 a year; his new position paid him $4,500.)

Wheaton's successor, Peters, had actively sought the Reporter's job with help from Wheaton's former publisher. Although Peters lacked Wheaton's scholarly inclinations, he possessed something far more valuable in a young editor—a strong entrepreneurial instinct. Scholarly disquisitions on the reported cases consumed costly paper and print; Peters knew that, at $7.50 per volume, Wheaton's reports had been beyond the reach of many lawyers. He also understood that busy lawyers preferred summary and synthesis to learned annotation. He figured that by trimming the size of the reports he could lower their price and sell more copies.

If condensed versions could sell more copies of current reports, they could also help sell past reports. Peters embarked on a condensed six-volume edition of his predecessors' twenty-four volumes, entitling it *Condensed Reports of Cases in the Supreme Court of the United States, Containing the Whole Series of the Decisions of the Court from Its Organization to the Commencement of Peter's Reports at January Term 1827.* He priced the abridged volumes almost 75 percent below Wheaton's volumes.

The *Condensed Reports* enjoyed great commercial success. But Peters's profit was Wheaton's loss, and with the market for his own volumes shrinking, Wheaton turned to his former law partner, Elijah Paine, to file suit against Peters. The suit alleged copyright infringement and sought an injunction and accounting of profits from Peters. After a two-year standoff between the court's two judges, the case went against Wheaton. Wheaton then promptly retained—via Paine—his old friend Daniel Webster to argue the appeal. In late September 1833, Wheaton sailed back to America from Liverpool to assist in the case.

Wheaton's complaint asserted rights under both the Copyright Act and the common law. Although the statutory period of protection for *Wheaton's Reports* had not yet expired, he pleaded the common law count as a precaution against a ruling that he had failed to comply with all of the Act's formal requirements for protection, including the deposit of copies of his reports with the Secretary of State within six months of publication. Strictly speaking, the Supreme Court did not have to address the common law count, but the Justices found the prospect of harrowing the ground already plowed in *Millar* and *Donaldson* too tempting to be lost for small technical reasons.

The Supreme Court delivered its decision on March 19, 1834. As dutifully reported in Volume 8 of *Peters' Reports*, the Court ruled that, once a book is published, the Copyright Act displaces the common law and becomes the exclusive source of rights in a published work. Writing for the majority, Justice John McLean echoed Justice Yates's dissent in *Millar v. Taylor:* "The argument that a literary man is as much entitled to the product of his labor as any other member of society, cannot be controverted. And the answer is, that he realizes this product by the transfer of his manuscripts, or in the sale of his works when first published." Justice Smith Thompson, dissenting, invoked Justice Mansfield: "Every one should enjoy the reward of his labor, the harvest where he has sown, or the fruit of the tree which he has planted . . ." However much it voiced the English discourse, *Wheaton v. Peters* was at bottom a distinctively American decision, representing a victory for federal over state power.

Wheaton v. Peters ultimately went off on a technicality. The trial court had held that the Copyright Act's deposit requirement was mandatory and that Wheaton's failure to make a timely deposit of his reports in the local district court had forfeited his copyright. Since it was not clear to the Supreme Court Justices that Wheaton had in fact failed to comply with the deposit requirement, they reversed the trial court's decision and remanded the case for another trial on the question. Wheaton prevailed at the retrial, and Peters appealed. Wheaton died while the second appeal was pending; Peters died less than a month later. Peters's estate settled the lawsuit by paying $400 to Wheaton's estate.

Congress's comprehensive copyright revision of 1870 was a turning point. One change was to move registration of copyright from the federal district courts to the Library of Congress; another was to require two deposit copies of each copyrighted work—one as evidence of registration (a practice started by the Stationers' Company in the sixteenth century), the other for inclusion in the Library's collection. Thanks largely to the deposit requirement, the Library quickly grew from the fifth largest in the country to the first; by 1897, when it moved into its spacious new quarters, the Library of Congress held 840,000 volumes, close to half acquired through copyright deposits.

Under the vigorous leadership of Ainsworth Rand Spofford, the Library of Congress became the center of copyright activity in the America. Thorvald Solberg, a library employee since 1876, became a nationally recognized copyright expert; when a separate copyright department was created in the Library in 1897, he was appointed the first Register of Copyrights. Solberg set an activist example followed by virtually every Register since; the Copyright Office today not only reviews registration applications for legal compliance but, working with authors and industry groups, proposes and drafts revisions of the law.

If the 1870 Act's encouragement of deposits to build the Library of Congress reflected a post-Civil War earnestness about preserving the national heritage, its extension of copyright to prohibit unauthorized new uses of literary works reflected a sensitivity to the burgeoning variety of American culture. Abridgments such as Peters's *Condensed Reports* signaled a new trend in publishing and in copyright. Increasingly, instead of making a knockoff copy, like Donaldson's edition of *The Seasons*, writers and publishers used a copyrighted work as the springboard for a new work—an abridgment or a translation—the second author mixing his labors with those of the first. With the emergence of a vital American literature—the works of James Fenimore Cooper, Washington Irving, and Nathaniel Hawthorne joining the more humble spellers, dictionaries, and law reports that were copyright's first and most common objects of protection—new markets emerged for the exploitation of original literary works, first in the form of translations and dramatizations, and eventually in sound recordings, motion pictures, and television.

Although these cases at first involved no technology newer than the printing press, they transformed copyright's central issue from the abstract question whether copyright was a natural right, to a more concrete anticipation of the problems posed by new technological uses of copyrighted works. To ask, as these cases did, whether copyright entitles the author of an English-language novel to enjoin a publisher from issuing an unauthorized German translation is, at bottom, like asking whether the novelist is also entitled to control the use of his novel in motion pictures or television productions based on it.

An 1853 case pitting Harriet Beecher Stowe against a writer who had translated *Uncle Tom's Cabin* into German without her permission raised these issues directly. The 1831 Copyright Act then in force in the United States was silent on the question of translations. The court chose to read the Act narrowly, as protecting only the "precise words" that clothed Stowe's ideas and not their transformation into another language. "I have seen a literal translation of Burns' poems into French prose," wrote Justice Robert Grier, "but to call it a copy of the original, would be as ridiculous as the translation itself." The 1870 Act reversed this result, and brought copyright into the new literary age by requiring translators—as well as those who would dramatize a work—to obtain the original copyright owner's consent.

The new generation of copyright cases also reflected a shift in concern over decisional power. Where *Wheaton v. Peters* addressed the allocation of copyright power between the states and the federal government, the new cases tested the allocation of decisional power between Congress and the federal courts. Their pattern soon characterized relations between the courts and the Congress in copyright's encounters with the unanticipated technologies of the Industrial Revolution. When an author sued for infringement of copyright because his work had been exploited by a new technology, should the court read the Act strictly, against the author, leaving him to the protracted process of obtaining support for legislative action, or should it be more expansionist and read the Act broadly to embrace the new realities?

Photography was the first new technology to challenge American copyright law. Could an image created by the reflection of light off a chemically treated plate qualify as a "Writing" of an "Author," as the Constitution required? Congress evidently thought so, for in 1865 it amended the Copyright Act expressly to add photographic prints and negatives to the classes of copyrightable works. Twenty years later, the Supreme Court first addressed the constitutionality of this action.

Napoleon Sarony, a noted New York photographer, sued the Burrow-Giles Lithographic Company for infringing his copyright because they had copied his photograph of Oscar Wilde. (The photograph showed Wilde seated, with one carefully positioned hand supporting his head, the other resting on an elegantly bound volume on his knee.) Burrow-Giles had reproduced and sold 85,000 copies of the picture without Sarony's consent. The Supreme Court quickly dismissed the printer's argument that, because it consisted of images, not words, a photograph could not be a "Writing" of the sort the Constitution intended. Maps and charts were similarly not "Writings" in any literal sense, the Court observed, but they were included in the first American Copyright Act, a law that had been passed with the support of many who had helped frame the Constitution.

Burrow-Giles's second argument was more nettlesome: "A photograph being a reproduction on paper of the exact features of some natural object or of some person, is not a writing of which the producer is an author." The notion that photographs are mere mirrors of reality, not artistic creations on their own, troubled Justice Samuel Miller. Only five years earlier, in the *Trade-Mark Cases*, Miller had written for a unanimous Supreme Court that copyright could not constitutionally protect symbols or devices used to advertise goods, because they were neither original nor creative; they were not "the fruits of intellectual labor."

Nonetheless, Miller, again writing for a unanimous Supreme Court, now upheld Sarony's copyright on the ground that the photograph was art, not commerce. Copyright might be unavailable for ordinary snapshots, he wrote, but Sarony's picture clearly showed the photographer's creativity. Sarony had made the photograph "entirely from his own original mental conception, to which he gave visible form by posing the said Oscar Wilde in front of the camera, selecting and arranging the costume, draperies, and other various accessories in said photograph, arranging the subject so as to present graceful outlines, arranging and disposing the light and shade, suggesting and evoking the desired expression, and from such disposition, arrangement, or representation, made entirely by plaintiff, he produced the picture in suit."

Sarony was hardly a ringing declaration in support of those who viewed copyright's cup as always half full. Nor did it offer an indiscriminate welcome to products of the new technologies. The Court's decision hinged on the assumption that Congress and the courts could confidently distinguish between works that were sufficiently artful to qualify for copyright and those that were not. Even here, the Court's opinion failed to dispel the doubt left by the *Trade-Mark Cases* that a commercial product, no matter how artful or popular, could qualify for copyright.

These ambivalences ultimately came to the Supreme Court of Justice Oliver Wendell Holmes, Jr. Holmes was no less rhetorically gifted, self-confident, or persuasive than Lord Mansfield. And, like Lord Mansfield, Holmes was no stranger to copyright. Four years before he heard his first copyright case on the Supreme Court, the Court had unanimously ruled that a popular work by Holmes's father, *The Autocrat of the Breakfast Table*, had fallen into the public domain for failure to comply with a formal copyright requirement (the same requirement that had sent Henry Wheaton back to trial after his initial loss in the Supreme Court). Holmes, Jr., as executor of his father's will, was himself the plaintiff in that case, and the memory of the decision could hardly have inspired him to take a crabbed, technical approach to the Copyright Act.

Bleistein v. Donaldson Lithographing Co. was Holmes's first copyright opinion on the Supreme Court. The case, decided in 1903, was between two printers, the plaintiff claiming that the defendant had infringed its copyright by reproducing three posters it had prepared to advertise a circus. The trial court and appeals court had held for the defendant, following a long line of decisions, including the *Trade-Mark Cases*, that excluded advertisements from copyright. Holmes dispatched the precedents in his characteristically lapidary style: "Certainly works are not the less connected with the fine arts because their pictorial quality attracts the crowd and therefore gives them a real use—if use means to increase trade and to help to make money. A picture is none the less a picture and none the less a subject of copyright that it is used for an advertisement. And if pictures may be used to advertise soap, or the theatre, or monthly magazines, as they are, they may be used to advertise a circus."

Holmes's taste for popular theater and burlesque may have nourished this generous view. Copyright was not just for Boston Brahmins; even more, it was for the popular marketplace. To impose a refined legal standard might be to deny copyright to pictures "which appealed to a public less educated than the judge. Yet if they command the interest of any public, they have a commercial value—it would be bold to say that they have not an aesthetic and educational value—and the taste of any public is not to be treated with contempt. It is an ultimate fact for the moment, whatever may be our hopes for a change. That these pictures had their worth and their success is sufficiently shown by the desire to reproduce them without regard to the plaintiffs' rights."

The creativity criterion that the Supreme Court had adopted in the Oscar Wilde case offered a tempting dividing line between copyrightable and uncopyrightable subject matter, and would certainly have sustained copyright in the elaborate circus posters. But Holmes was concerned about the power such a litmus test would give to copyright purists. He added a now famous dictum: "It would be a dangerous undertaking for persons trained only to the law to constitute themselves final judges of the worth of pictorial illustrations, outside of the narrowest and most obvious limits. At the one extreme some works of genius would be sure to miss appreciation. Their very novelty would make them repulsive until the public had learned the new language in which their author spoke. It may be more than doubted, for instance, whether the etchings of Goya or the paintings of Manet would have been sure of protection when seen for the first time."

With the copyrightability of photographs established in the Oscar Wilde case, and with the copyrightability of commercial products upheld in *Bleistein*, it should have taken only a small judicial step for a court to uphold copyright in motion pictures. Nonetheless, when Thomas Edison sued a rival for copying a film that one of Edison's employees had made of the launching of Kaiser Wilhelm's yacht *Meteor*, the trial court ruled against Edison on the ground that the Copyright Act did not expressly cover motion pictures. In 1903, the appeals court reversed this ruling, holding that when Congress added photographs to the classes of copyrightable subject matter it must also have contemplated the prospect of movies: "It is not to be presumed it thought such art could not progress, and that no protection was to be afforded such progress." (Congress finally brought movies into the Act in 1912.)

It is one thing to hold that motion pictures qualify for copyright and that one film copied from another will infringe, quite another to hold that a motion picture that takes no more than its theme and action from a novel or short story will infringe the copyright in the literary work. Congress had by now overturned the *Uncle Tom's Cabin* decision and extended copyright protection against unauthorized translations and dramatizations. Was this legislative step to be read as inviting courts to read the Act broadly, to extend the copyright owner's control to encompass any work, in whatever format, that borrowed his expression? Or was it an injunction to draw the infringement line narrowly, covering no more than translations in book form or dramatizations in the form of a play?

Justice Holmes tackled the question in a case concerning an unauthorized motion picture based on General Lew Wallace's novel *Ben-Hur*. Rejecting the narrow approach taken in the *Uncle Tom's Cabin* case, he deployed a dazzling logic to sweep technological distinctions aside: "Drama may be achieved by action as well as by speech"; no one would deny that a pantomime based on a novel constituted a dramatizing of the novel; "if a pantomime of Ben-Hur would be a dramatizing of Ben-Hur, it would be none the less so that it was exhibited to the audience by reflection from a glass and not by direct vision of the figures—as sometimes has been done in order to produce ghostly or inexplicable effects." His conclusion: "Moving pictures are only less vivid than reflections from a mirror."

Holmes could have disposed of *Ben-Hur* on a simpler ground. Before making the film, the defendant had arranged for a screenplay to be written based on the novel. Since the screenplay was also unauthorized, and since it clearly constituted a dramatization under the terms of the Copyright Act, a decision for the plaintiff could easily have rested on the proposition that the screenplay infringed. Why, then, did Holmes choose to pursue a circuitous path through pantomimes and mirror images? The answer probably lies in his perception that an opinion that focused on the screenplay alone would leave an economically far more important medium—theatrical exhibition of films—outside the scope of copyright. In a word, here was *Bleistein redux*: a narrow statutory phrase, a hesitant Congress, and a Supreme Court Justice intent on building a bridge between copyright and popular culture.

The decision to focus not on *Ben-Hur's* screenplay but on its exhibition presented a possibly embarrassing problem: although, under the logic of Holmes's opinion, it was the film's exhibitors, not its producers, who infringed the copyright, only the producers, and not the exhibitors, were before the Court. Holmes seized on this paradox to expand the scope of copyright still further, accommodating the law to an environment in which, given the costs of pursuing many individual infringers, a copyright owner's only effective relief will be against the single person who made the infringement possible. By making the films available for exhibition, Holmes reasoned, the producers had effectively participated in the infringement and thus could be held as accomplices. "If the defendant did not contribute to the infringement it is impossible to do so except by taking part in the final act."

Musical compositions in traditional notated form had been protected by copyright since 1831. Anyone who copied musical notations would infringe the copyright. But the Copyright Act did not address the question of recorded music: Did the act of making a recording such as a piano roll or phonograph record infringe the copyright in the musical score? An answer to this question was not easy. It is one thing to locate the impress of an author's personality in a photograph or motion picture, quite another to detect it in the strips of paper dotted with an unintelligible array of tiny holes that animate mechanical pianos, or the even less intelligible grooves on a phonograph record.

The History of an Idea

Composers and music publishers had long acquiesced in piano rolls that copied their tunes. But as piano rolls and then phonograph records threatened to erode their income from the sale of sheet music, music copyright owners went to Congress for relief. They chose their moment well. In 1905 Congress had begun to overhaul the 1870 Copyright Act, and the composers and publishers saw to it that among the proposed amendments was one that would give them an exclusive right against the manufacture or sale of any "appliance especially adapted" mechanically to record musical compositions.

The player-piano manufacturers opposed the bill, but not for the expected reason. They had no objection to sharing revenues with the composers and publishers, they said; their complaint was that copyright protection against unauthorized recorded music would effectively give an industry-wide monopoly to the one pianola manufacturer that favored the bill—the Aeolian Company. Evidently anticipating a favorable judicial decision on the mechanical recording right, Aeolian had bought much of the soon-to-be-created mechanical recording rights from America's principal music publishers. The three-cornered dispute among Aeolian, the other pianola companies, and the copyright owners was one of the thorniest on the copyright revision agenda. A case relating to the issue—and financed by Aeolian—was making its way through the courts, and Congress was happy to postpone action on the bill until the Supreme Court acted.

White-Smith Music Publishing Co. v. Apollo Co. arrived in the Supreme Court during its 1907 term. Apollo, a manufacturer of player pianos and piano rolls, opened its brief to the Court by invoking *Wheaton v. Peters* for the proposition that copyright in the United States is strictly the creature of statute, and cited the *Uncle Tom's Cabin* case for the proposition that courts must apply the statute according to its literal terms. The Court, Apollo argued, was not free to expand the Act's scope beyond the statutorily prescribed "copies"—in the case of musical compositions, the "legible embodiment" of the composer's inscription of notes on a page. Since the piano roll embodied no more than an illegible scattering of tiny holes, it could not possibly be an infringing "copy." The music publishers, for their part, argued that a decision against them would violate copyright's purpose to protect "the intellectual conception in the compilation of notes which has resulted which, when properly played, produces the melody which is the real invention of the composer."

The Supreme Court ruled for Apollo in a decision that copyright scholars have since excoriated for putting technical niceties over artistic substance. Nonetheless, it showed a practical appreciation for the allocation of copyright power between Congress and the courts when dealing with popular new technologies. According to the Court, from seventy to seventy-five thousand of such instruments were in use in the United States in 1902, and from one to one and a half million musical rolls had been made that year. A finely tuned law was needed, not the blunt instrument of a judicial injunction that would disrupt the expectations of the thousands of people who owned pianolas.

Even Justice Holmes joined in the Court's decision. But his concurring opinion advised Congress in terms that left no doubt as to his notions of what it should do as a matter of good copyright policy. On principle, he wrote, anything that mechanically reproduces a musical composition's "rational collocation of sounds" ought to be held a copy, "or if the statute is too narrow ought to be made so by a further act," except, and here Holmes presumably had the Aeolian mo-

nopoly in view, "except so far as some extraneous consideration of policy may oppose."

The Supreme Court decided *White-Smith* on February 24,
1908; congressional hearings on the pending bills resumed
within a month and culminated with the addition in the
1909 Act of a copyright against the unauthorized mechanical
reproduction of musical compositions. Congress brought
phonograph records as well as pianola rolls within the new
law, and also took account of the feared Aeolian monopoly
by subjecting the right to a compulsory license. Once a
copyright owner authorized a pianola or record company
mechanically to copy his musical composition, any other
company was free to make its own recording of the composition by the simple expedient of paying the copyright owner
two cents for each record it produced.

Victor Herbert and John Philip Sousa, both famous and
popular composers of the day, had testified in favor of copyright protection from unauthorized pianola rolls and phonograph records. Aided by a music attorney, Nathan Burkan,
Herbert had filed a friend of the court brief in the *White-
Smith* case. Now, with Burkan's unstinting and often unpaid
help, Herbert and his musical colleagues turned to the problem of unauthorized public performances of their works,
which occurred in thousands of restaurants and dance halls
across the country. Their journey would share two features
with the evolution of the mechanical recording right: a transforming encounter with a new technology and a blessing
from Justice Holmes at a crucial moment.

Although Congress had granted a public performance right
to musical compositions in 1897, it was difficult to enforce
the right. First, the 1909 Act provided that for an unauthorized performance to infringe copyright it had to be not only

public but also "for profit." Concerts where admission was charged were an easy case. But was background music in a restaurant played "for profit"? Second, unlicensed performances went on in cabarets, dance halls, and restaurants in virtually every city, town, and village in the United States. To police each infringing performance and file lawsuits against them would likely cost more than any damages that might be recovered. It would cost fifty dollars to collect ten.

What was needed was a collaboration between writers and publishers in a test case that would liberally define the "for profit" requirement, and an institution that could police and collect royalties from all over. There was precedent for such organized efforts in Europe, where musical performance rights had existed somewhat longer. In 1851, French composers, authors, and publishers had formed the Société des Auteurs, Compositeurs et Editeurs de Musique to license and collect royalties from musical performances. Although SACEM had attempted to enlist American composers by opening a New York office in 1911, the idea of collective action languished for lack of interest until the idea of an American performing rights society took hold in the fertile mind of Nathan Burkan.

On a rainy October night in 1913, nine composers and music publishers joined Burkan for dinner in a private dining room at Lüchow's Restaurant in Manhattan to organize an American performing rights society. (Thirty-five had been invited. The empty places at the table must have seemed an ominous portent for the venture's prospects.) One of the composers present was Raymond Hubbell, who later wrote an informal history of the fledgling society. According to Hubbell, Victor Herbert was the first to arrive, "as always, energetic, bubbling over, in a hurry," boosting any dampened spirits. When one of the publishers, an Englishman, suggested that the society be called the American Society of Composers, Authors and Publishers, one of the songwriters pointed out that it was customary in America to refer to "Authors and Composers" in that order, not the reverse. The Englishman was not impressed: "Oh, but think of what a good cable code the first letters make the other way." ASCAP was born.

After four months spent organizing ASCAP and plotting its course, the composers and publishers set themselves to the task of getting New York cafés and restaurants, for a start, to take a performance license from it. Lüchow's was the first licensee; for fifteen dollars a month, the restaurant now had the right to perform the works of any ASCAP member. Other restaurants were less tractable, and eventually turned to their own organization, the New York Hotel and Restaurant Association, to resist any claim that their performances were "for profit."

By summer 1914, with their attempted negotiations going nowhere, it became clear to ASCAP that a lawsuit was their only option. Nathan Burkan filed suit on behalf of John Philip Sousa's publisher against the Hilliard Hotel Company for performing Sousa's march "From Maine to Oregon" in the dining room of Manhattan's Hotel Vanderbilt. The trial court held for the publisher, but the appeals court reversed; the hotel's performance, the court reasoned, could not be considered "for profit," since restaurant patrons had not been charged an admission fee.

Undaunted, Burkan was back in court two months later, this time representing Victor Herbert. The defendant was Shanley's, a Manhattan theater-district restaurant whose floor show included a performance of "Sweethearts" from a Herbert musical. Following the precedent of the earlier Sousa appeal, the trial court ruled against Herbert. The appeals court affirmed, setting the stage for an appeal of both cases to the United States Supreme Court.

The Supreme Court delivered its opinion on January 22, 1917, Justice Holmes writing for a unanimous Court. As he had in the *Ben-Hur* case, Holmes declined the defendant's urging to read the Copyright Act narrowly. Congress, he wrote, had not intended the "for profit" limitation to deprive composers and writers of the full measure of their works' economic value. "If the rights under the copyright are infringed only by a performance where money is taken at the door they are very imperfectly protected. Performances not different in kind from those of the defendants could be given that might compete with and even destroy the success of the monopoly that the law intends the plaintiffs to have."

Holmes quickly perceived the value in these performances. The only question was who got to reap that value—the author or the user. "The defendants' performances are not eleemosynary. They are part of a total for which the public pays, and the fact that the price of the whole is attributed to a particular item which those present are expected to order, is not important. It is true that the music is not the sole object, but neither is the food, which probably could be got cheaper elsewhere. The object is a repast in surroundings that to people having limited powers of conversation or disliking the rival noise give a luxurious pleasure not to be had from eating a silent meal. If music did not pay it would be given up. If it pays it pays out of the public's pocket. Whether it pays or not the purpose of employing it is profit and that is enough."

With the principle established that commercial performances are "for profit," ASCAP could now turn to its central mission: collecting royalties from licensees and distributing them to the society's members. From the beginning, the central collecting mechanism was a blanket license that would give the licensee *carte blanche* to perform any composition in the ASCAP repertory as often as it wished for a flat fee. The appeal of a blanket license would necessarily turn on the comprehensiveness of the ASCAP repertory; no licensee wanted to be put to the bother of determining whether a song it chose to play was in ASCAP's repertory, nor did it want to run the risk of guessing wrong and facing an infringement lawsuit from an unaffiliated composer or publisher.

To build up a comprehensive repertory, ASCAP's bylaws provided that any composer, author, or publisher who met specified standards could become an ASCAP member. Once admitted, the member would transfer to ASCAP the right to license the nondramatic performance of his works. (These nondramatic performance rights are called "small" performance rights, to distinguish them from the "grand" performing rights, dramatic rights involved when the composition is performed as part of an opera or musical comedy. Composers and publishers retained the grand performing rights.) ASCAP would sample licensee performances to determine how frequently individual works were played and, after deducting overhead expenses, would apportion the license revenues among its members, following a distribution schedule that accounted for the relative popularity of the members' works.

The logic of ASCAP's operations, particularly the logic of the blanket license, is the logic of monopoly: only by gathering all copyrighted compositions into its repertory could ASCAP give users a blanket license that would enable them to perform any musical composition without fear of a lawsuit. But monopoly breeds discontent—and not only in the U.S. Congress and among the antitrust enforcers in the Justice Department. Many of ASCAP's newer members chafed under a royalty distribution calculus that they believed the founding members had weighted against them. But with no competing organization to join, they had to make do with the system devised by ASCAP's older members. It took a new technology—radio—to ignite this discontent and radically transform ASCAP's way of doing business.

ASCAP's board correctly perceived that the revenues to be earned from radio broadcasts would soon dwarf the revenues coming from restaurants and dance halls. Its first step was to establish a legal precedent that radio performances were both public and for profit. The radio stations turned to their newly formed trade group, the National Association of Broadcasters, to defend their interests. The broadcasters' position was essentially that because no members of the public were present in the broadcast studio, the performances could not be considered public, and because the public paid nothing to listen to radio, the performances were not for profit.

ASCAP prevailed in the first round. Suing the Bamberger department store, which operated and sponsored programs on a New Jersey radio station, the composers and publishers won a decision that radio performances are made publicly for profit. Relying extensively on Holmes's opinion in the *Herbert* case, the court ruled that the plaintiff need show only that the radio station intended to make an indirect profit from its program, and that Bamberger's broadcast advertisements helped it to do so. Justice Holmes's foresight had saved the day for the music industry.

As radio became more and more successful in the 1930s,

ASCAP tried to capture a larger share of its revenues through increased license fees. Since musical performances took up the great bulk of broadcast time, it argued, this was only fair. Moreover, radio performances were cutting into its members' other sources of income, notably record and sheet music sales. The broadcasters countered that ASCAP's practices constituted monopolistic price fixing and that, in any event, radio play actually boosted sales of sheet music and records by giving them what amounted to free advertising. (When Bamberger made this argument, the court had astutely observed: "Our own opinion of the possibilities of advertising by radio leads us to the belief that the broadcasting of a newly copyrighted musical composition would greatly enhance the sales of the printed sheet. But the copyright owners and the music publishers themselves are perhaps the best judges of the method of popularizing musical selections.")

Prompted by the broadcasters, the Justice Department filed an antitrust suit against ASCAP, charging that the society had destroyed competition between members and nonmembers and, indeed, members themselves. One major publisher soon entered the fray, withdrawing its works—almost one-third of ASCAP's catalogue—and voicing the old complaint that ASCAP management discriminated in favor of members of its old guard. Neither initiative was conclusive. After ten days of hearings, the Justice Department, possibly sensing defeat, requested an adjournment. After eight months of failed efforts to license their works on their own, the defecting publishers returned to the ASCAP fold. Like round one, round two belonged to ASCAP.

With their ASCAP licenses set to expire on December 31, 1940, and anticipating still higher royalty demands, the broadcasters unveiled a new strategy: they would enter the music licensing business themselves, in direct competition with ASCAP. In September 1939, they announced the formation of Broadcast Music, Inc., a corporation to be owned exclusively by broadcasters. When ASCAP delivered its new—as expected, higher—royalty proposals, they refused to negotiate and turned instead to building up BMI's music catalogue. They had little success in luring away ASCAP members—managing to sign only one major publisher—but they did manage to sign on new composers by paying them advances against future royalty payments. BMI also bought up the rights to Latin American music that ASCAP had previously ignored.

On January 1, 1941, ASCAP music went off the air across the United States, except on a few independent radio stations that had renewed on ASCAP's terms. Instead of the old standards and new pop songs of the day, radio listeners were now treated to reworked versions of public domain classics—Stephen Foster was especially popular—and to the endlessly repeated Latin beat of "Frenesí," "Perfidia," and "Amapola." Advertisers, the sole source of broadcast revenues, stood by the stations. ASCAP members were reeling from a double blow: they not only suffered dwindling royalties from radio but also lost revenues from the sale of records and sheet music, establishing the empirical truth of the broadcasters' claim that radio broadcasts in fact boosted music sales.

The broadcasters had called ASCAP's bluff and won. By August 1941, ASCAP was ready to capitulate, and by October agreed to a new contract that would bring its members only a little more than one-third of the royalties it had proposed less than two years earlier. Yet, by 1943, ASCAP had bounced back, collecting more revenues than it had before the black-out.

Amid the tumult of these radio wars, the Justice Department had not lost sight of ASCAP. In late December 1940, just as ASCAP's contracts with the stations were about to expire, the government announced its intention to file an antitrust action—this time suing *both* BMI and ASCAP—alleging eight violations of the Sherman Antitrust Act. A month later, BMI settled with the government by signing a consent decree whose provisions would control its future operations. ASCAP held out for another month before it, too, agreed. The decree prohibited ASCAP from interfering with any member who issued a nonexclusive license to a user who wished to deal with the member directly. And just as a compulsory license had been used to curb the Aeolian Company's monopoly decades before, the decree as later amended permitted a prospective licensee to apply to federal court for binding determination of a "reasonable fee" in the event it could not agree with ASCAP on the cost of a license.

As one looks back over ASCAP's evolution from the small dinner meeting at Lüchow's to its present operations in a sky-scraping command center that overlooks Manhattan's Lincoln Center, collecting more than $300 million annually for distribution to more than fifty thousand members, one element of its success stands out: the central role that artists have played in its daily work. Since the 1940s, a succession of writers and composers have served as ASCAP's president, among them Morton Gould, Hal David, Deems Taylor, and Otto Harbach. Writers sit alongside publishers on its board. When an infringement lawsuit is filed, it is often in the composer's name, not the publisher's, and never ASCAP's. Hardly a congressional hearing that touches on the interests of the Society's members goes by without testimony from a popular songwriter or composer.

It is no accident that ASCAP keeps creators to the fore. When Parliament rebuffed the Stationers who hoped to keep their perpetual monopoly, the publishers knew their best chance for success lay in an alliance with the writers, and in admitting writers into their formerly exclusive Company. The appeal is emotional—public sympathy is stirred by the image of an artist struggling alone in his garret—but also rational. Copyright is, after all, about authorship, about sustaining the conditions for creativity that enable an artist to create out of thin air and intense, devouring labor an *Appalachian Spring*, a *Sun Also Rises*, a *Citizen Kane*.

Until the middle of the twentieth century, the presence of authors, the idea of authorship, dominated every encounter between copyright and a new technology: the "new, harmonious, characteristic, and graceful picture" that Justice Miller detected in Napoleon Sarony's portrait of Oscar Wilde; the "personal reaction of an individual upon nature" that Holmes found in the *Bleistein* posters; the significant presence of Victor Herbert and his exuberant supporters in the case against Shanley's Restaurant.

Copyright's next major encounter with a new technology, a 1968 lawsuit against unauthorized photocopies, might well have replayed ASCAP's encounters with radio—a test case orchestrated to dramatize the plight of artists, a spirited band of authors and publishers in league against unabashed pirates. But when the Williams & Wilkins Company, a Baltimore publisher, sued the National Library of Medicine and the National Institutes of Health for photocopying articles from its medical journals, no writers—and not even other publish-

ers—cheered it on. The outcome of copyright's pivotal encounter with the photocopy machine turned not on the popular appeal of creative artists or on the popular scorn for
pirates. The case depended on the energy and will of one
very stubborn man, Williams & Wilkins's president, William
Moore Passano.

CHAPTER THREE

Fifty Dollars to
Collect Ten

An heirloom portrait hangs in the living room of William Passano's nephew Mac Passano. The portrait is of Joseph da Passano, painted on the eve of his departure from Genoa to establish a new home in the United States with his wife and young son. The painting shows Passano, the son of a distinguished judge of the Ecclesiastical Court of Rome, seated at a reading table. The angle of his resting arm draws the viewer's eye to a scrap of paper at his elbow on which is written the enigmatic slogan "A mad Passano am I."

Compiling the family history four generations later, William Passano speculates. Joseph da Passano was by all accounts the black sheep in the family. Did these curious words mean that he left Genoa because of an angry falling-out? Or was he simply questioning his sanity in sailing for America? "My hunch is that it was a combination of the two," his descendant writes. Joseph da Passano died in 1865 in Baltimore, Maryland, and was buried there in Greenmount Cemetery.

In January 1963, William Passano became a Baltimore publisher, taking over as president of the Williams & Wilkins

Company, the medical publishing house that his father had
founded in 1909 as an offshoot of the family printing business. Passano was trained as an engineer, and his career had
thus far been in the printing operations, overseeing the installation of new Linotype machines, testing out a new letter-
press, hiring a research and development director to monitor
new printing technologies. Nothing had prepared him for a
new technology that would soon complicate his life as a publisher: the Xerox 914 photocopier. Introduced in 1960, the
high-speed machine offered performance—the production of
good, cheap, and quick copies—that outstripped the prevailing technology.

The business of publishing is as far removed from the business of printing as racetrack betting is from feeding horses.
Printing is a business of labor and physical commodities. The
field of play with your competitors is level: facing the same
expenses for labor, ink, paper, and type, your rival is hard put
to undersell you. Publishing is far riskier. Book publishing is
an act of faith in your ability to pick enough winners to
compensate for the all-too-frequent books that lose money.
You must have faith, too, that the law will protect you from
poachers who try to reprint your successful books without
any of the risk of the less popular ones, and without paying
royalties to your authors.

When an employee told Passano that the United States
government's National Library of Medicine was photocopying tens of thousands of articles from Williams & Wilkins
journals each year without payment or permission, Passano's
reaction was rage. "I don't want to be looked on as an easy
mark. You know the tramp that puts a mark on a gatepost to
say, 'The people who live here are soft touches?' I don't want
anybody to think I'm one, that they could take my money

and get away with it." Passano's son put it bluntly. His father, he said, "would spend fifty bucks to collect a ten-dollar bill on a matter of principle." Passano senior did not disagree.

To William Passano's engineer mind, there was something more than profitability at stake. Something, Passano thought, was out of balance, not true, if copyrighted works could be copied without compensation to their producer. But he was torn. He knew he had to speak out, but he was terrified at the prospect. (Many years later, when writing the family history, he traced his stage fright to an incident in his earlier career as a printer when his father still controlled the company. He had been invited—he thought—to present a paper on wage incentives to the American Society of Mechanical Engineers in New York City. "Just before I mounted the podium to deliver my address, the chairman said to me: 'Oh, I thought we had invited your father to be on this program.'") And, indeed, no little madness surrounded his decision to take on the library community over the issue of photocopying—speaking to library groups, proselytizing fellow publishers, and testifying before Congress. For a publisher, particularly a medical publisher, to confront libraries on this issue meant entering into battle with his best customers. Not surprisingly, no other medical publisher joined Passano. At one point, when his prospects of success were riding an exhilarating upward curve, he heard the chilling rumor that medical libraries across the country were about to boycott his entire list of journals.

Passano's claim that the libraries had no business making unauthorized photocopies had two centuries of copyright behind it. As new technologies such as the phonograph, radio, and television opened up new markets for copyrighted works, Congress regularly, if belatedly, moved to extend the law's reach to encompass the new use. But Passano had to reckon with a circumstance more powerful than law or history, and it soon plunged the American copyright system into disarray. Phonograph records and radio and television broadcasts all trace to sources that are easily located and easily licensed. But the photocopy machine is different: here for the first time was a technology that enabled people to make copies in hundreds of thousands of offices and libraries across the country, outside anyone's sight or control. Would Congress impose liability—would courts enforce copyright—when the revenues owing for each copy were so low and the threat to privacy was so high?

Passano's training as an engineer taught him that an unsound structure will sooner or later collapse on itself. Early on, he had seen the weakness of the business world's discrimination against women. One of his first steps on taking the helm at Williams & Wilkins was to appoint a woman to head a company department. " 'Oh, Mr. Passano, you can't do that. Men won't take orders from a woman.' I said, 'You're crazy as hell. They've been taking orders from women ever since they were in diapers.' " But after waiting for years for the anomaly of uncompensated photocopying to collapse, he began to worry that here was one structural defect that might not fall of its own weight. Librarians refused to change their photocopying practices unless Congress or the courts told them to. Congress, embroiled in the efforts to revise the 1909 Copyright Act, was in stalemate. Testifying before the Senate's intellectual property subcommittee, Passano quoted a favorite verse from Oliver Wendell Holmes, Sr.:

> *In vain we can old notions fudge*
> *And bend our conscience to our dealing.*

Copyright's Highway

*The Ten Commandments will not budge
And stealing will continue stealing.*

Passano remembered the subcommittee chair, Senator John McClellan of Arkansas, looking at him as if to say "Why, you smart-ass!"

Rebuffed by a recalcitrant library community and ignored by an impassive Congress, this great-great-grandson of a mad immigrant from Genoa, this first-time Baltimore publisher, finally turned for relief to that uniquely American institution for resolving great issues of public policy: a lawsuit. On February 17, 1968, shrugging off cautions from fellow publishers, he filed a complaint for copyright infringement against the National Library of Medicine and the National Institutes of Health. The adventure ultimately brought him and his cause to the Supreme Court. According to a *Washington Post* headline, the controversy topped the Supreme Court business list. "Few cases in recent years," it observed, "have held the challenge and consequences of the copyright case called Williams & Wilkins Co. vs. The United States."

Because William Passano had chosen to sue the government, he filed his complaint in the Court of Claims, the trial court for copyright lawsuits against the United States. The complaint was stamped, docketed, and assigned to Trial Commissioner James F. Davis, one of only two intellectual-property experts among the court's fifteen commissioners. Davis supervised the parties' pre-trial motions and discovery of evidence, presided over the trial, made findings of fact, and ultimately determined who won the case. Thirty-six years old, Davis was the court's youngest commissioner, but his record was very strong: in more than a year on the job, Davis had never yet been reversed by the Court of Claims in an intellectual property case.

The National Library of Medicine houses a vast collection of medical books and journals. A librarian's library, it makes its holdings available to other libraries through interlibrary loan. Between 1957 and 1961, the library "lent" 352,262 works, and most of these, 301,528, were photocopies. The National Institutes of Health, a conglomerate of specialized medical research institutes, have their own library, from which they, too, made photocopies for the research staff—close to a million pages a year by 1970. Neither institution was indifferent to its potential copyright liability. As early as 1957, NLM director Martin Cummings predicted that it was "possible, if not indeed probable, that the years would bring, sooner or later, a test of the issue in the courts."

On April 28, 1967, Passano wrote to Cummings that Williams & Wilkins would allow the National Library of Medicine to copy its journal articles for a license fee of two cents per page. Cummings referred the letter to the General Counsel of the Department of Health, Education, and Welfare and promptly replied to Passano that he would in the meantime suspend photocopying from the company's journals. A definitive reply came a month later: "It is our opinion that this long-standing practice of making photocopies for scholarly purposes represents a fair use of the copyrighted materials, and I am, therefore, giving directions to the Library staff that our service be continued as in the past."

A prominent physician with a long career as a tuberculosis researcher, Martin Cummings had been a high-level administrator at the National Institutes of Health for three years before moving to the National Library of Medicine as director in 1964. After three years at the library, in which his principal project was to oversee the installation of a new computer system—years that Cummings later recalled as "joyful"—he suddenly found himself the government's point man in the photocopying controversy, acting not only for the National Library of Medicine but also for the National Institutes of Health. For six frustrating years, the dispute occupied the center of his time.

At about the time Cummings's second letter arrived, Passano was attending a copyright conference in New York City, where, by chance, he met a lawyer named Alan Latman. Latman had studied copyright at Harvard Law School under the legendary Benjamin Kaplan and, like so many of Kaplan's students, could not resist copyright's elegance and eccentricities. In twenty-one years of practice, he had happily contrived never to stray far from the field.

Although Passano did not know it at the time, Latman was also the country's leading expert on the doctrine of fair use that would dominate his case against the two government libraries. Fair use is a judicial safety valve, empowering courts to excuse certain quotations or copies of copyrighted material even though the literal terms of the Copyright Act prohibit them. In a study that he wrote for the Copyright Office in 1958, analyzing every court decision on fair use in the United States—the doctrine has a long lineage, tracing back to the 1841 decision in which Justice Joseph Story reflected on copyright's metaphysics—Latman observed that courts had allowed writers to quote copyrighted material for many reasons and in a wide variety of settings, from parodies to news reporting and scholarly research. This fair use copying also encompassed copies made for criticism or private study. But on the question of library photocopying, the courts and the commentators were silent, and Latman in his study had not speculated.

Custom is important in fair use. If copyright owners regularly acquiesce in certain copies or quotations made by others, that alone is evidence that the use is reasonable and fair. One custom that could be expected to overshadow the Williams & Wilkins lawsuit was the Gentlemen's Agreement entered into between library and publishing representatives in 1935 to express their understanding about the permissible scope of copying under the technologies of the day. The Agreement stated that, so long as a library made no profit from the practice, it could make a "single photographic reproduction" of copyrighted material for a scholar who stated in writing that he wanted it "in lieu of loan of such publication or in place of manual transcription and solely for the purposes of research."

Within a week of Passano's encounter with Latman, he asked him whether he would be interested in representing the company in a copyright action against the National Library of Medicine. Latman responded immediately and enthusiastically. Eben Perkins, the company's regular lawyer, who had no expertise in copyright law, told him that they hoped Latman would take the laboring oar.

On July 11, when Passano and Perkins went to Bethesda to present their formal demand for compensation to the National Library of Medicine, Cummings knew something that they did not. In 1962, one of his staff members had surveyed the copyright ownership of the journals in the library's collection and ascertained that most of the copyrights were owned by professional medical societies; only a few of the journals from which the library most frequently copied were owned by commercial publishers like Williams & Wilkins.

The staff also calculated that, at two cents a page, the total royalties the library would have had to pay Williams & Wilkins over a three-month period would amount to no more than $300. Since the library was copying about a million pages from the journals of all publishers each year, a two-cent royalty would cost a total of $20,000. "That's peanuts," Cummings said. "We could afford to pay that and get this whole thing resolved."

Why, then, did Cummings reject Williams & Wilkins's proposed two-cent license? Here, Passano and Perkins may have misjudged the director. Although Cummings's entire professional career before coming to Washington had been as a physician and medical researcher, he now identified strongly with his fellow librarians. "When I discussed this with other library directors and with other people interested in the problem," Cummings recalled, "they pointed out that we were only a small piece of the whole library community, and that if this two-cents-a-page charge was applied nationally, it would amount to a rather large sum and that it would be unfair for the National Library of Medicine to agree to this without other academic and public libraries being involved." On June 24, 1967, the Association of Research Libraries voted to support Cummings's continued photocopying in the face of Williams & Wilkins's demands. Five days later, the American Library Association also voted to support the National Library of Medicine.

Misjudgments of character ran both ways. If Cummings thought that Passano's computation of the paltry royalties to be earned from a two-cents-per-page levy would dissuade him from suing, he misjudged a man who would spend fifty dollars to collect ten. Cummings may also have made a misstep in inviting Passano and his staff to observe the library's photocopying activities. "That would prove to be a hell of a mistake, because I think if they hadn't come, they probably wouldn't feel as strongly as they did. They saw a factory type of photocopying that might have really concerned them. When you saw all of this photocopying taking place in a sophisticated setting I guess you could be worried that it might affect you economically."

Seeing the library's virtual printing plant may have fueled Passano's rage, but he also had a tactical reason to sue the government. Congress had recently amended the Judicial Code to subject the United States government to copyright infringement actions for the first time. The provision offered a remedial twist that Latman and his partner, Arthur Greenbaum, found compelling. In contrast to copyright actions against private infringers, which gave prevailing copyright owners injunctions almost as a matter of course, section 1498 of the Judicial Code prohibited injunctive relief against the government, relegating the copyright owner to "recovery of his reasonable and entire compensation." Here was a provision that meshed perfectly with William Passano's design, not to stop the flow of scientific information, but only to obtain fair compensation for the use of his property.

A suit against the two libraries did present tactical difficulties. To compute "reasonable compensation," Williams & Wilkins would have to identify, specifically, each of thousands of journal articles that the libraries had photocopied. Latman concluded that the best strategy was to divide the lawsuit in two. In the first part he would seek simply to establish that unauthorized photocopying constitutes copyright infringement, a principle that he could establish with a handful of infringements as well as with hundreds. The second part could then compute the libraries' monetary liability by counting the number of infringements overall, by which time, he hoped, the libraries would be ready to enter into a license covering all Williams & Wilkins journals, thus saving the company the expense of tallying individual infringements.

But what if the two libraries refused to take a license for any articles other than the ones Williams & Wilkins had specifically identified in its complaint? As a backstop, Latman struck on an innovative ploy. He would allege seven specific infringements in his complaint and then, in an eighth omnibus count, would allege "upon information and belief" that the defendant had "infringed other copyrights of plaintiff by copying, printing, reprinting, publishing, vending, and distributing works which are respectively the subjects of said copyrights." He would request "leave of the court to amend this petition upon discovering the identity of such other works." Williams & Wilkins would have done its duty with the seven samples of copied articles; it would be up to the government to document the vast remainder of infringements in the course of pre-trial discovery.

The problem with Latman's omnibus eighth count was that the Copyright Act did not permit fishing expeditions. Unlike class action suits—in which a single purchaser injured by a defective product can sue the manufacturer on behalf of a vast, unnamed class of individuals who bought the same product—the Copyright Act required the copyright owner to produce a copyright registration certificate for each and every work that he claimed was infringed. Without a registration certificate, the court would have no jurisdiction even to entertain the claim.

The court granted the government's motion to dismiss the omnibus count, and Latman quickly added a new eighth count alleging infringement of a specific article, "Occlusion of the Hepatic Veins in Man," which had appeared in the journal *Medicine*. With the company's claims thus trimmed, Greenbaum joked, a victory in the Court of Claims would mean "we probably would have collected eight dollars and twelve cents."

With only eight journal articles in suit, it now became even more important for Latman to show that the government libraries had copied each article more than once. So far, Passano had only been able to identify instances in which the libraries had made a single copy—precisely the conduct sanctioned by the 1935 Gentlemen's Agreement. Latman urged him to assign someone on his staff to review the NLM records for evidence of multiple copying, but Passano resisted. In part he was concerned that the effort might backfire. The court, he thought, might seize on scattered evidence of multiple copying as an excuse to split the difference, holding that multiple copies infringed copyright but that single copies were fair use, leaving him with no relief against the principal problem, which was photocopies made one at a time. Also, Passano could find no one to volunteer for the job. "We have decided," Passano wrote to Latman, "that we would prefer to have our suit against the Government sink or swim on the basis of whether or not making a single copy of an article is a copyright infringement."

Preparing a major case for trial is rarely a smooth ride. The dismissal of the omnibus eighth count and Passano's decision not to document multiple copying were sharp jars to Latman's development of the case. More jolts were to come. In June 1968, the Supreme Court handed down *Fortnightly v. United Artists Television*, holding that a cable television system did not infringe copyright when, without the copyright owner's permission, it retransmitted motion picture broadcasts from local television stations. Latman knew there was a difference between the Copyright Act's grant of the exclusive right "to perform"—the issue in *Fortnightly*—and its grant of the right "to copy"—the issue in *Williams & Wilkins*. But the Supreme Court speaks only rarely on copyright issues and, when it does, creates a legal climate that extends far beyond the facts in the single case. The climate created by *Fortnightly*, exempting a new technological use of copyrighted works, was hardly congenial to Passano's claim. "The spirit, if not the letter, of the decision will certainly be cited against us at some stage," Latman wrote to Eben Perkins.

There was more unsettling news. With the deposition of witnesses well under way, Latman reported to Passano in May on the latest deposition, and "even more interesting"—dropping the bombshell as lightly as he could—briefed him on his discussions with government officials about the federal grants that supported most of the research published in Williams & Wilkins journals. "We have now learned that beginning July 1, 1965 the Public Health Service Policy contained an express provision granting a non-exclusive royalty free license to the Government to copy and make other use of publications resulting from a Public Health Service Grant." Five of the eight works in Williams & Wilkins's complaint had been written under Public Health Service grants, one after the adoption of the policy that expressly gave the government the right to make free copies, the others at a time when, the government alleged, it had an implied license to make free copies. Focusing on the claim of an implied license, Latman asked: "Was the express language granting the Government a license added to *change* prior practice or merely to codify it?"

A lawyer could answer the question one way or the other, but lawyerly distinctions between express and implied licenses were little comfort to Passano. From the beginning, he had been looking to the future, not the past, and for the future, an express provision giving the government a royalty-free license to copy articles produced from government-sponsored research meant that the National Library of Medicine and the National Institutes of Health would be free to copy up to three-quarters of the articles appearing in his journals.

Fifty dollars to collect ten might not be a bad bargain if it won a legal judgment ensuring many times that amount in future photocopying revenues. But the new Public Health Service policy was a fact that, however painful, an engineer's mind could quickly grasp. There was no nuance here, no shade of gray. The hand that gives can also take away, and the government had taken away the prospect of return on the great proportion of articles appearing in Williams & Wilkins journals. "I rather suspect that had we known before we entered suit against the Government what we know now," Passano wrote to Latman, "we might never have gone forward with the suit." Passano listed, as the first of several options, "to drop the suit here and now rather than throw good money after bad."

Latman took a week to consider the situation and consult with his partners. On June 10 he wrote Passano to propose that they continue the lawsuit, add new counts to cover articles that had not been supported by the Public Health Service, and fight the government's claim that it had an implied license to copy pre-1965 Public Health-supported research. He suggested that they should drop the count for the article published after 1965, however, since it was clearly subject to the express license. Passano acceded, but was still concerned about good money following bad. "We also agreed," he wrote Latman, "that we would be most welcome to an out-of-court settlement, but that the chance of this approach being productive was too slight in my opinion to justify spending time or money on it."

With the clear outlines of his case being eroded at the edges by legal niceties, Passano began to consider an engineering solution against the event that his legal claim should fail. In April 1970 he showed Latman a copy of *Medicine* that he had printed on a special "noisy" paper that could not be reproduced on a photocopier. Passano expressed the hope that "we will not be obliged to enter into this antimissile missile type of operation but that we can win our lawsuit instead." Latman thought the paper was "terrific except that it is a little difficult on the eyes." Four years later, while the case was pending in the Supreme Court, Passano was still holding on to his engineering "ace in the hole."

At the moment, technological fixes were the least of Latman's concerns. He had to map a legal theory for the case, a metaphor that, investing the facts with legal consequence, would impel Commissioner Davis to decide for his client. The easiest, textbook approach was the *prima facie* case. Section 1(a) of the Copyright Act made it unlawful to copy a copyrighted work without the copyright owner's consent; each Williams & Wilkins article was a copyrighted work; and the National Library of Medicine and the National Institutes of Health had copied the articles without Williams & Wilkins's consent. The government's only avenue of escape was the doctrine of fair use. But after more than a century on the books, fair use had never been applied by any court to excuse the copying of an *entire* work.

Logically compelling as the *prima facie* case might seem, Latman and Greenbaum knew they needed something more if their case was to survive the intense scrutiny of Commissioner Davis and of every federal judge who would review his decision on appeal. The two lawyers knew—Passano would not let them forget—that they had to explain not only that the law was behind them but that justice, too, compelled their cause. Latman and Greenbaum would make the *prima facie* case, but they would also argue that photocopies were a substitute for a purchased Williams & Wilkins journal, giving researchers free something for which Passano had paid and at the same time depleting his subscription base. Greenbaum recalled: "We devoted a lot of effort to developing an explanation as to how Williams & Wilkins would be hurt by the copying that was being done by the National Institutes of Health and the National Library of Medicine." Paid experts were not needed, for "Bill Passano himself could explain how he was being hurt. He knew the business better than anybody else; he could explain it."

The trial in *Williams & Wilkins v. The United States* began on Wednesday, September 9, 1970, in an elegant walnut-paneled courtroom in the Court of Claims courthouse on Lafayette Park, across from the White House, and continued for six days. Latman's first witness was William Passano, a tall and balding man whose tortoiseshell glasses and brush mustache softened an otherwise austere mien.

Latman led his client through a description of his company and its operations. Williams & Wilkins, Passano explained, was a division of the Waverly Press, the family printing company whose printing revenues substantially exceeded its publishing revenues. Williams & Wilkins produced most of its thirty-seven journals jointly with professional medical societies. The American Society of Immunologists, for example, sponsored the *Journal of Immunology*. A medical society typically would appoint an editorial board which would decide what manuscripts the journal would publish. "Then they turn the manuscripts over to the publisher and we take it on from that point." The societies and Williams & Wilkins split the profits between them.

Latman turned to the heart of his case. "Getting back to large-scale photocopying, what potential effect, if any, do you find such photocopying by libraries to have?" Passano answered that the effect of photocopying was to stunt the growth of his subscription list and the sale of reprints and back numbers.

LATMAN: Any other potential effects that you can think of?
PASSANO: Well, when it is uncontrolled, it has the effect of eliminating the possibility of receiving a royalty on the photocopy, which we receive from certain concerns.
LATMAN: Is there any relationship between this potential effect, that you just mentioned, and the cost involved in the publishing of the journal?
PASSANO: The so-called preparation costs, that is the cost involved before a single copy, runs anywhere from fifty to sixty-five percent of the total cost, and with periodicals of this nature, whose subscription list numbers three thousand, five thousand and so forth, anything which reduces the number of subscribers spreads that preparation cost over a decreasing number of copies and therefore the cost per copy, the unit cost, goes up very steeply.

Here was the message that, in one forum or another, Passano had been preaching for five years to Congress, to librarians, to publishers, to anyone who would listen. This was the message on which Latman had pinned the theory of the case: unrestricted photocopies substitute for journal subscriptions, driving up costs and driving away subscribers.

Thomas Byrnes had been in the Justice Department's Patent Section less than five years when he was assigned to defend *Williams & Wilkins v. The United States*. After six years as a practicing chemist, deciding, "I just didn't want to be in a laboratory for the rest of my life," Byrnes had enrolled in night law school—"four years, five nights a week, two hours a night." Like Commissioner Davis a member of the highly specialized patent bar, Byrnes now spent most of his time representing the government in patent lawsuits. *Williams & Wilkins* was his first copyright case. "I suspect that Mr. Brown, who was the chief of the section at that time, probably said to me, 'Do you want to work on this case?' And I said, 'Yes.' At that time I always said, 'Yes.' I was always eager for work."

Byrnes recalled that when the case came to him he saw it as just another case against the government. His complacency was no comfort to Martin Cummings, who knew that the plaintiff's lawyers were pursuing their client's cause as the case of a lifetime; he was concerned that Byrnes was not. "It took us months to show him the potential effect this would have."

Byrnes may have failed at first to appreciate the significance of the case, and compared to Latman and Greenbaum, he may have been underexperienced and understaffed. (Byrnes handled the case entirely on his own.) But none of these handicaps was evident from his cross-examination of William Passano. Well prepared, direct at times, shrewdly oblique at others, Byrnes deftly led Passano down not one but two treacherous paths, both starting from the proposition, in which Passano concurred, that the number of photocopies had increased since the introduction of Xerox machines.

BYRNES: And would it be fair to say that if Xeroxing or providing of photocopying is having any detrimental effect on your business, that detrimental effect has been steadily increasing?

PASSANO: In my opinion, that would be a fair statement, yes.

The key phrase was "any detrimental effect." Did detrimental effect mean a decline in the journals' profitability? If so, Passano would have to show that profits had in fact declined. Or did it mean Williams & Wilkins had lost subscriptions? If so, Passano would have to show that the company had in fact lost subscriptions.

Byrnes placed the financial statements for the *Journal of Immunology* before Passano, pointing out that the journal showed a net loss in 1959 and 1960, but net profits in all succeeding years, paying off the 1959–60 deficit in 1963. Half this payment came from the share of the profits allocated to the American Society of Immunologists.

BYRNES: In 1969, the *Journal of Immunology* made $16,900 and in 1970 you expect to make $45,000 and in 1971, you expect to make $50,000, is that right?

PASSANO: I expected it when those figures were written. Since then I have had less optimistic expectations.

BYRNES: In any event, it is quite an improvement, isn't it?

PASSANO: Yes, sir, it is.

Byrnes then turned to the question of lost subscriptions. He showed Passano the statement he had made before the Senate

Patent, Trademark, and Copyright Subcommittee in April 1967: "We know that photocopying has already seriously reduced the income of most of the thirty-nine periodicals which we publish."

BYRNES: Do you know in dollars and cents, how much damage photocopying has done to the journal, *Medicine*?

PASSANO: I don't measure it in dollars and cents. I measure it in the number of subscriptions.

BYRNES: And what is your form of measurement in terms of subscriptions?

PASSANO: Twofold. One is the behavior of the subscription list from year to year and the other is the amount or the number of subscribers, compared to what might be considered a reasonable potential for that journal.

BYRNES: What is a reasonable potential for *Medicine*?

PASSANO: I think three or four times the present circulation.

BYRNES: On what fact do you base that?

PASSANO: Because it is admitted to be one of the finest medical journals in the world.

Even as he spun out these threads, Byrnes intermittently circled away from the question of photocopying's detrimental effects, drawing Passano into another corner of his web. Passano conceded that Williams & Wilkins did not pay its authors for their contributions. Indeed, in many cases, journal authors themselves paid the publisher "page charges"—a fixed fee for each page in excess of a predetermined maximum—to publish their articles. Did Williams & Wilkins, Byrnes asked, pay *any* compensation to its authors? The answer was: "We published their material."

What kind of publisher, Byrnes was implying, does not

have to pay royalties to its authors? What kind of publisher, other than a vanity press, requires its authors to pay to be published? The premise behind copyright law is that property rights are needed to encourage authors and publishers to make the judgments and take the risks essential to the creation and dissemination of new works. How much risk was Williams & Wilkins taking if the medical societies shared the risk and authors helped pay the way? As for editorial judgment, Passano testified that medical societies or independent editors ran the day-to-day operations of most of his journals, selecting and editing articles on their own.

Indeed, Byrnes may have been suggesting, Williams & Wilkins was not a publisher at all, only a printer. Its financial statements, which he introduced into evidence, showed that the journal's largest expenditure by far was for printing. (The 1966 statement for the *Journal of Immunology* showed that, of the journal's $92,306 expenses, close to $77,000 went to printing, mailing, and overhead costs; only slightly more than $14,000 went to "redaction" and "editorial" costs.) Was Williams & Wilkins anything more than an adjunct to the Waverly Press, merely a vehicle for channeling regular work to the much larger printing company that controlled it?

It was now Byrnes's turn to put on his case. Over five days, he questioned one witness after another, directing their testimony toward the four factors that American courts traditionally weigh in determining copyright fair use: how many words out of the total text the defendant had copied (in Passano's favor, the libraries had copied entire articles); the nature of the copyrighted work (scientific works were especially favored in fair use); the purpose of the use (the libraries' aid to medical research and patient care was another point in Byrnes's favor); and, most important, the effect of the photocopying on the market for the copyrighted work (Passano's faltering testimony on lost subscriptions would help Byrnes).

Some of Byrnes's witnesses were authors of the articles involved in the lawsuit; others had consulted Williams & Wilkins articles in the course of research or patient care. Two messages rang through: Williams & Wilkins authors did not object when libraries made uncompensated photocopies of their works; and researchers and physicians wanted quick and easy access to journal articles. For a physician to have to wait for a reprint—and reprints were not always available—might mean vital information was unavailable at the very moment it was needed to save lives. The message, though extreme at times, had the insistent ring of truth. Alan Latman had little success in shaking Byrnes's witnesses on cross-examination.

Byrnes's final witness, Robert Blum, took aim at the fourth fair use factor, the alleged harm that library photocopying had inflicted on Williams & Wilkins's markets. A former government economist, Blum took the stand armed with statistical tables and multicolored charts. He testified that, beginning in 1960, the total number of subscriptions for three of the journals in suit, *Medicine*, the *Journal of Immunology*, and *Gastroenterology*, had increased more rapidly than had the nation's scientific and technical personnel, and that the growth in Williams & Wilkins's revenues exceeded the growth in the country's gross national product and its expenditures on scientific research.

This was the first time Latman had seen Dr. Blum's charts and tables, and he now had to make a quick strategic decision whether to cross-examine Blum on the spot or to ask for a continuance to enable him to study the testimony and data. Latman lacked the background in economics and statistics that he thought he might need to rebut Blum's premises and conclusions. But, a savvy litigator, Latman looked for cues from Commissioner Davis, and Davis seemed to be saying that cross-examination would be fruitful right now. With an eye to the trial record as it might be read by an appeals court, he said he would give Latman the time he needed to prepare for Blum's examination, but added, "My impression is, however, on the basis of what I have been able to tell from following his testimony, that there is nothing in those analyses—and I could be wrong about this, but I don't see anything which you could not, within a very short time, be able to cross-examine the witness on. I'm not an economist nor a mathematician, and I followed that along fairly well, and even saw questions on cross-examination that I would like to ask." Here was an invitation Latman could not refuse, effectively an offer of aid from the court if he should fail to ask Blum what Davis thought were the right questions.

After a ten-minute recess, Latman began his cross-examination, questioning Blum from several directions, probing for a weak spot—in Blum's choice of indexes against which to measure Williams & Wilkins's performance, Byrnes's possible role in shaping his expert's testimony, Blum's lack of data on the quantity of library photocopying. Finally, he struck on a line of questioning that Davis, who had by now actively joined in, clearly thought was important: Would Blum be able to determine whether Williams & Wilkins had lost any revenues from photocopying if the economist in fact had data on the amount of the libraries' photocopying? Blum demurred. Without actual data, he could not answer the question.

Davis interjected: "The fact of the matter is that if all you have is what you have now, plus X number of copies of Williams & Wilkins' publications made in a given year, you can't really draw any conclusions from that, alone, with respect to whether the company would have done better or worse?" Latman picked up the commissioner's line of questioning. "How can you ever tell—ever—that any particular instance or instances comprising X would or would not have resulted in the loss of a particular form of revenue by Williams & Wilkins? How can you ever tell?"

If Thomas Byrnes's cross-examination of William Passano on the first day of trial had undercut the publisher's claim that free photocopies substituted for journal subscriptions, Latman's cross-examination of Blum on the last day of trial had at least put the facts into equipoise. So far, no one had proved that photocopying did or did not harm Williams & Wilkins.

It was now hours past the trial's usual 4:30 p.m. adjournment time. "I remember warning everybody that we were going to try to end on a particular date, no matter how long it took," Davis recalled, "sort of half in jest. Well, it turned out we got to the time and we weren't done. We took a break at about 4 p.m. and I called the lawyers aside and I said, Look, we're going to go 'til we're done." Davis missed his goal of finishing on September 16 by twenty minutes. The trial adjourned at 12:20 a.m. on Thursday, September 17.

By 9 p.m. the fans and air circulation in the building had shut down. Davis took off his robe and encouraged the lawyers to take off their jackets. Byrnes read into the record a portion of Passano's deposition where he had said it was possible to prove that photocopying eroded a journal's subscription base only by asking: Would you have subscribed to this journal if you couldn't photocopy? As it turned out, the answer to the question had dangerous implications, and Latman now put Passano on the stand one last time.

LATMAN: Mr. Passano, do you still believe that it is only possible to prove the point of erosion on journals as a result of photocopying by asking people, "Would you have subscribed to this journal if you couldn't photocopy it?"

PASSANO: No, I don't.

LATMAN: And can you explain the basis for your change of view?

PASSANO: Well, the basis is that I don't believe that asking them would prove the point.

LATMAN: Why not?

PASSANO: I don't think that you could unscramble the eggs; that some people wouldn't know, and they might speculate. I don't think that you'd get any really reliable information by asking people.

Byrnes decided not to cross-examine Passano, but even at this late hour, the energetic, youthful commissioner was fascinated. "Just a minute. Do I understand this, Mr. Passano. What you are saying is that their answer as to whether they would or would not might not be one which would be carefully considered at the time asked, or what? I don't quite follow you on that."

Passano answered, "It would be the kind of a questionnaire that I don't believe they would be in a position to answer with accuracy. They might think they would; or they might say something that they think would be the appropriate thing to say, rather than maybe what they felt in their souls; but even if they said what they really believed, if the time came to act, there's no guarantee that they would act that way."

Davis seemed satisfied. But, violating the cardinal rule for a witness never to volunteer information not asked for, Passano went on, "When I answered that question the way I did, it was on the basis of a telephone survey that we made after one of our journals failed, and we thought it was due to photo-copying, and out of eighteen people that we talked to, one man said that was why he didn't resubscribe, because he could get photocopies; and I thought, 'Well, if we had carried that survey across the land, perhaps this would really tell the story.'"

Latman tried to interrupt, but Passano continued, "The more I thought about it, the more I realized that that would not be a very valid conclusion to reach." Latman finally suc-ceeded in stopping his client. "Do you think the question re-quires too much speculation on the part of the answerer?"

"That's right."

But Passano's elaboration intrigued James Davis. "What was it about this journal that failed, and the calls that were made? What was it?"

PASSANO: We called the people who had subscribed, in Balti-more, who did not renew their subscription, to ask them why they didn't; and there were eighteen calls, as I remem-ber it, that we made to the Baltimore ex-subscribers, and one of the eighteen said he didn't do it because he could go to the library and get it photocopied.

DAVIS: Do you recall what were some of the other reasons from the other seventeen?

PASSANO: It was no longer of use to them, or the laboratory had it; or they had moved and we weren't able to get them. There were all kinds of answers like that.

DAVIS: I see. All right. Thank you.

Suddenly, at the very end of a six-day trial, here was one piece of testimony, one shred of fact, that might finally shed light on the question whether photocopying had deprived Williams & Wilkins of subscriptions. Would Commissioner Davis treat the response of one out of eighteen ex-subscribers as evidence that photocopying had materially reduced subscriptions, or as evidence that photocopying had only a trivial effect? Or would he treat it as evidence not worthy of weight one way or the other? What did he mean by his noncommittal "I see"?

In the months following the trial, Latman and Byrnes drafted briefs detailing the applicable law and pored over the trial transcript and exhibits to prepare their proposed findings of fact for Commissioner Davis. By January 7, 1971, Latman told his client, he had "gone through the 1,300 pages and exhibits" and "abstracted the several hundred nuggets which we knew were there." By spring, Byrnes had submitted his papers; Passano spent five single-spaced pages on a detailed, critical analysis of them. Briefs from several *amici curiae*, friends of the court, joined Latman's and Byrnes's papers—the Association of American Publishers and the Authors' League of America on the plaintiff's side, the American Library Association, the Association of Research Libraries, the Medical Library Association, and the American Association of Law Libraries on the defendant's side.

James Davis issued his decision in *Williams & Wilkins v. The United States* on February 16, 1972. To puncture the suspense that had mounted in the seventeen months since the end of the trial, Davis stated his conclusion in the very first paragraph of his sixty-three-page opinion: "I hold that defendant has infringed plaintiff's copyrights and that plaintiff is entitled to recover 'reasonable and entire compensation' as provided by §1498(b)."

After wading through several peripheral issues, Davis centered on the heart of the case: the libraries' claim that their photocopying was fair use. Davis wrote that the libraries' activities met none of the four criteria of fair use, and focused on the pivotal fourth one, about market effect: "The photocopies are exact duplicates of the original articles; are intended to be substitutes for, and serve the same purpose as, the original articles; and serve to diminish plaintiff's potential market for the original articles since the photocopies are made at the request of, and for the benefit of, the very persons who constitute plaintiff's market." Conceding that "it may be difficult (if not impossible) to determine the number of subscription sales lost to photocopying," he insisted nonetheless that "the fact remains that each photocopy user is a potential subscriber, or at least is a potential source of royalty income for licensed copying." He added, "There is evidence that one subscriber cancelled a subscription to one of plaintiff's journals because the subscriber believed the cost of photocopying the journal had become less than the journal's annual subscription price."

Davis could have written a short opinion to accompany his findings of fact or, indeed, no opinion at all. "I remember when I got done with the findings in this case I was kind of worn out. It was a big job. I wasn't sure whether I was going to write a full opinion or not. The more I thought about it I said 'I've got to write a full opinion.' The case was too important, and there were too many things to be said." Also, "I felt very strongly that I was correct on the case. I really thought I had the answer. So I wanted an opinion and I knew I was going to have trouble upstairs."

Davis's concern about "trouble upstairs" underscored another possible strategic misstep in Passano's decision to sue the government. The Court of Claims's only business was to decide claims against the government, and this truncated jurisdiction may have systematically biased at least some judges in the government's favor. "My perception may not have been accurate," Davis recalled, "but I thought there were some judges up there who would be very unlikely to make the government pay anything in a case like this." One of the court's intellectual leaders, Oscar Davis, may have had such leanings. "The only time I ever had any tanglements with him on appeal was in situations where I was holding for a plaintiff against the government and he thought I shouldn't have."

Four months before, in October 1971, Passano, Latman, and Greenbaum had drafted a settlement proposal to present to NLM and NIH in the event they won a favorable ruling. Now Latman presented it to the government: under their plan, the two libraries would, upon payment of a license fee, be free to photocopy articles from Williams & Wilkins journals for patrons in the regular course of library operations. The license fee would be five cents for each journal page, multiplied by one of three numbers chosen at the libraries' option: the number of text pages that Williams & Wilkins planned to publish in each journal at the beginning of the subscription year; the number of pages actually photocopied by the libraries; or the number of pages that both parties agreed represented the approximate number of pages photocopied by the libraries.

The Justice Department's frosty reply came on March 20. "We regret to inform you that your offer to settle the above entitled suit has been found to be unacceptable. The Government agencies against which this suit is principally directed have indicated a strong desire to seek a final judicial resolution of the issues presented by this case. While we do not wish to foreclose forever the possibility of settling this case, further offers to settle similar to the one specified in your letter will not be received favorably."

It is hard to negotiate in a vacuum, without a counterproposal, but a vacuum is all that the government offered.
Nonetheless, Passano and his lawyers spent two more months
laboring on a new proposal that drastically simplified the earlier licensing scheme and lowered its cost. *All* libraries, not
only the two government libraries, could subscribe to
Williams & Wilkins journals at an institutional rate somewhat
higher than the rate for individual subscribers; this higher rate
would confer a blanket license to make single copies for library patrons; interlibrary loans would be charged at five
cents per page. (Because libraries already kept records of interlibrary loan transactions, there would be no added recordkeeping burden.)

A June conference between the parties and their lawyers
was inconclusive. In August, Latman suggested to the Justice
Department that his client might give up payment for interlibrary loan copying so long as the libraries paid the institutional rate for subscriptions—"with the understanding that
the right to copy contemplated by such institutional rate will
be referred to as a replication right and not as a license to
copy." This bit of lawyer's word play—a "replication right" is
somehow different from a "license"—tried to accommodate
three competing realities: the libraries' unwillingness to give
in to the principle that their activities required a license; Passano's commitment to the principle that his rights were being
violated; and Nixon-era price controls that arguably prohibited rate increases that did not embody some additional value
for library subscribers.

Passano pressed these increasingly attenuated proposals on
an intransigent Justice Department in part to establish the

principle of compensation that had driven his cause from the beginning. But he was also concerned about his company's bottom line. The effect that organized library opposition could have on a single publisher had become painfully clear to him during the spring and summer of 1972. The NLM had in March sent a memo to their grantees telling them that NLM grant funds could not be applied to license payments to publishers without its prior approval, and throughout the summer Williams & Wilkins got letters from medical libraries pointedly declining to renew their subscriptions at a rate that included a license to photocopy. In August, Passano showed Latman copies of letters from five Illinois medical school libraries—"all identical and all declaring a moratorium on subscribing to our journals." He added that his company president, Charles Reville, had received a telephone call that morning from their agent in Texas "telling him that some of the big medical libraries in his territory had received instructions, he thinks from Dr. Cummings, to boycott our journals."

In late September, Greenbaum told Passano that the government had rejected their last proposal and would not agree to any fee that, however nominally, was connected to photocopying. The prospect that the NLM would fail to renew its subscriptions was even more unsettling than a boycott by medical school libraries. "As for *Index Medicus*"—the major authoritative bibliographical listing for all medical journals—"the rule is that if NLM doesn't have a particular journal in its collection it is not listed." Not wanting to lose his client's listings in this critical reference tool, Greenbaum added that he and the government's representative had agreed that the listing problem "could probably be solved by a gift of the volumes to NLM."

In early October, Passano capitulated. Writing to "Customers and Friends," he concluded that "in order to allow the NLM and all libraries to subscribe to Williams & Wilkins journals at increased rates and include them in *Index Medicus*, we now accept the NIH-NLM position. Our new institutional rates, which we shall continue to request, shall have no connection whatever with a license to photocopy, implied or otherwise. In short, libraries may continue to supply their users with royalty-free, single-copy reproductions of Williams & Wilkins journal articles as they have done in the past." In the same spirit, Passano added, "We are, again without prejudice, withdrawing our proposal for the five-cents-per-page inter-library loan fee until the appeal of our case has been heard."

The Court of Claims handed down its decision five months later. Like Commissioner James Davis, Court of Claims Judge Oscar Davis stated the court's decision "in this ground-breaking copyright infringement action" in his very first paragraph, holding "the United States free of liability in the particular situation presented by this record."

Boiled down, the Court of Claims decision rested on three propositions: "First, plaintiff has not in our view shown, and there is inadequate reason to believe, that it is being or will be harmed substantially by these specific practices of NIH and NLM; second, we are convinced that medicine and medical research will be injured by holding these particular practices to be an infringement; and, third, since the problem of accommodating the interests of science with those of the publishers (and authors) calls fundamentally for legislative solution or guidance, which has not yet been given, we should not, during the period before congressional action is forthcoming, place such a risk of harm upon science and medicine."

On the central question of harm to the copyright owner, the court rejected Commissioner Davis's premise that, when in doubt, copyright's cup should be viewed as half full rather than half empty. "It is wrong to measure the detriment to plaintiff by loss of presumed royalty income—a standard which necessarily assumes that plaintiff had a right to issue licenses. That would be true, of course, only if it were first decided that the defendant's practices did not constitute 'fair use.'" The court also dismissed Passano's informal survey of Baltimore subscribers. "This small number of purported cancellations is *de minimis* in view of the more solid and detailed proof as to the health of plaintiff's journals and the increase in their subscription lists."

The decision was 4–3, with Chief Judge Wilson Cowan among the dissenters. Writing a separate dissent, Judge Philip Nichols observed that, however hedged, "the decision will be read, that a copyright holder has no rights a library is bound to respect. We are making the Dred Scott decision of copyright law." He also objected that the court had seriously tampered with James Davis's fact findings, including his finding that at least one subscriber had cancelled because of the availability of photocopies. Facts, once found by a trial court, are not supposed to be disturbed on appeal.

Passano was vacationing when he got news of the Court of Claims decision. "I made up my mind that was the end. I wasn't going to pour more good money after bad." Apart from the uncounted hours he had himself invested in the case so far, he had by now paid his lawyers more than $100,000. Shrewdly estimating the effect of the Court of Claims decision on other publishers, who would see it as establishing a

05/12/2018

Item(s) Checked Out

TITLE: Profit from your idea :
BARCODE   33029101002913
DUE DATE   **06-02-18**

TITLE: Copyright's highway :
BARCODE   3 3029 03521 6514
DUE DATE   **06-02-18**

TITLE: The copyright handbook :
BARCODE   33029103908752
DUE DATE   **06-02-18**

What can one book do?
Change the life of a first grader.

Donate today and help us put books in
the hands of first graders.

www.bigdayofgiving.org/saclibraryfriends

Thank you for visiting the library!

Sacramento Public Library

www.saclibrary.org

Terminal #   6

dangerous precedent that threatened their livelihood, he laid down an ultimatum. "I've had enough. I'm not going to go any further."

Other publishers had reason to be concerned about a precedent holding that library photocopying was fair use. Studies in the 1960s showed that more than a billion photocopies of copyrighted materials had been made in 1967 and that the number was increasing; the great majority of these were made without permission from the copyright holder. It might take no more than a strong advocate and an appealing set of facts to persuade a court that wholesale photocopying of educational materials for classroom distribution—chapters from textbooks, instructional materials, teaching aids—has as great a claim on fair use as library copying.

Curtis Benjamin, president of McGraw-Hill and chairman of the Copyright Committee of the Association of American Publishers, got Passano's message; quickly he organized a fund to take the case to the Supreme Court, ultimately collecting $110,000. Passano was pleased, of course, but he had little reason to think the Supreme Court would take the case. The Court accepts only a small fraction of the appeals that come to it, and rarely copyright appeals. Its only previous brush with the fair use doctrine had involved the comedian Jack Benny's claim that his radio parody of the motion picture *Gaslight* constituted fair use, a case that on appeal had resulted in a 4–4 tie (Justice William O. Douglas had declined to vote); the effect of the tie was to leave the lower court decision against Benny standing. Also, the Court already had another case before it involving a transcendent question of access to information. On May 24, 1974, Special Prosecutor Leon Jaworski had asked the Supreme Court to review a lower court order requiring the disclosure of tapes that President Richard M. Nixon had made in his office, tapes whose disclosure ultimately led to the President's resignation later that year.

Nonetheless, and against all odds, on May 28, 1974, the Supreme Court granted *certiorari*—agreed to hear the appeal—in *Williams & Wilkins v. The United States*. (Three days later, it granted Jaworski's petition for *certiorari*, too.) Barbara Ringer, Register of Copyrights, whom Latman had known since his days in the Copyright Office, wrote him: "Between you and the President this Court will cover the spectrum; the rights of those who refuse to show to anyone and those who'll strike off copies virtually at will." Passano was even quicker off the mark, telling Latman two days after the grant of *certiorari*, "Of course, it always seemed to me that they should hear the case, but with the pressure being put on the Court to deal with the matter of the Nixon tapes, I was afraid that our case might be pushed aside. I assume you will pass the word on to Curtis Benjamin since he should start raising money in earnest now."

Latman and Greenbaum injected an almost military discipline into their preparation of the appeal. On December 12, five days before the scheduled Supreme Court hearing, Latman rehearsed his argument in his firm's conference room before a mock court of New York lawyers. He had already assigned specific points to the six *amici* in order to avoid duplication. Passano reviewed all the briefs, reading some to his wife. "I told her," he wrote Latman, "I did not see how our case could have been better handled from start to finish than it was. She said that the main reason for this success is the fact that you and I work so well together and hold each other in such respect and esteem. I know that goes for my feelings toward you and I suspect that it is reflected in your feelings toward me. Win, lose or draw it has been a great experience."

The government's lawyer in the Supreme Court is the So-licitor General, a Justice Department official who practices only before the Supreme Court. In most cases, the Solicitor General delegates argument to one of his assistants. But Solic-itor General Robert Bork decided that *Williams & Wilkins* was one of the handful of important cases he would take on personally. Just two days before the argument, Bork invited Martin Cummings to meet to discuss the case. Cummings went with his deputy, Harold Schoolman. The meeting sobered the idealistic Cummings. "I put all my soul into this for all these years, and nobody really gives a damn now. Here's a guy who's going to go up and defend our position and I didn't know what he was going to say. He didn't tell us. I just felt totally left out."

On the morning of December 17, Chief Justice Warren Burger called the case. "We will hear argument first in Num-ber 73-1279, The Williams & Wilkins Company against The United States. Mr. Latman, you may proceed whenever you are ready."

Basketball-player tall, with wavy dark hair and deep, ringed, friendly eyes, Latman walked from counsel's side table where he had been waiting nervously—this was his first Supreme Court argument—to the lectern at the long table before the bench. Chief Justice Burger faced him directly, flanked, four on each side, by the Court's Associate Justices. "Mr. Chief Jus-tice, and may it please the Court: This is an action for copy-right infringement against the United States Government."

Although neither the Court nor Congress had ever ex-pressly endorsed the fair use doctrine, there was little chance that, after a century on the books, it would be discredited by the Supreme Court. The challenge for Latman was to tease out a golden thread from the mass of fair use decisions, a bright line that would preserve the fair use exception but would also prohibit photocopying on the scale conducted by the two government libraries. The tip of the golden thread, waiting to be drawn out, was that, in every fair use case thus far, courts had excused only copies of fragments, never copies of a whole work. Fair use, Latman now argued, "applies to an incidental use by one writer of someone else's work in terms of a portion of the work, but never so as to constitute an effective substitute for the original work."

At its best, argument in the Supreme Court is a conversation between the advocate and the Justices. The advocate tells the story of his client's case, shaping and coloring the account to steer the Court toward a favorable decision. If a Justice interrupts the telling, and invariably they do, the lawyer will, as subtly as he can, try to bring the Court back to his story, the theory of his case. Justice Potter Stewart broke into Latman's presentation. If cheap and easy photocopies revolutionized library copying practices beginning in the early 1960s, did this have any perceptible effect on the level of subscriptions to Williams & Wilkins journals? "Did the libraries, the National Library and the National Institutes of Health, before the early 'sixties, subscribe to more copies of your publications than they now do?"

Latman understood the import of Stewart's question all too well. If widespread photocopying had not reduced subscriptions, what harm had Williams & Wilkins suffered that it could complain of now? He had to choose between a mild response—even if subscriptions did not decline, nonetheless they did not *grow*—and a more ambitious theory: The mere fact that one use does not substitute for another is no reason to excuse it. For example, even though motion pictures do not substitute for the novels on which they are based, no one would argue that a motion picture producer might take the characters, plot, and dialogue from a novel without the copyright owner's permission.

Latman chose the less ambitious course. "I don't believe the record is conclusive one way or another. I don't think I can say they subscribed to more." Taking the *Journal of Immunology* as an example, Latman noted that, in an era of transplants and cancer research, the interest in immunology has "mushroomed." If subscriptions merely stayed at previous levels, this would suggest that library photocopying had substantially undercut his client's prospective profits.

Somewhere in the pile of briefs was a reference to the Library of Congress. Chief Justice Burger wanted to know what that Library's practice was. "Could you clarify, if you know, what is their practice with respect to furnishing full copies?" Latman answered that the practice of the Library of Congress "is in direct and dramatic contrast to the libraries in question." Under Library of Congress policy, "copyright material will ordinarily not be copied without the signed authorization of the copyright owner."

Justice Thurgood Marshall followed up. "Does that apply to the public? Does it also apply to Members of Congress?"

At the heart of most cases that reach the Supreme Court is a single question and a single answer that can spell success or failure for a party's claim. The question rarely turns on strict legal theory. Usually it goes to plain, practical circumstance, to the lives sometimes even of Supreme Court Justices. This is the question that a good advocate will discuss with his colleagues to the point of fatigue, that he will ponder if he awakes at 4 a.m., the question that, he hopes, one fortunate morning, stepping into the shower or snapping his briefcase shut, will suddenly yield a definitive answer.

Such a question had lurked in *Williams & Wilkins v. The United States* from the beginning. On the morning of the Supreme Court argument, over breakfast with his partner, Greenbaum, and their new associate, Carol Simkin, the three finally settled on an answer. If the answer did not shine with the blazing light that would ensure victory, it might at least forestall defeat.

Justice Marshall's question whether the Library of Congress's restriction on photocopying applied to the public and to members of Congress looked to Latman as if it was heading in the direction of the feared question. It was one thing for Williams & Wilkins to ask that copyright prohibit systematic copying by large institutions such as the National Library of Medicine and the National Institutes of Health. But if the two libraries could be charged for copying for the public, wouldn't Latman have to concede that individual members of the public could themselves be enjoined? And if individuals could be enjoined, where would copyright liability end? Do Supreme Court Justices infringe copyright when they make copies of law-review articles for their research?

Latman's answer, that the Library of Congress policy applied to the public, appeared to satisfy Justice Marshall. Having averted the feared inquiry about private copying, Latman took advantage of a break in the questioning to return to his central theme. "If a fellow writing a biography of Howard Hughes decides to borrow from an earlier work on the same subject and his work wouldn't substitute for your getting and reading the original, he is and was in the *Rosemont* case held to be using it fairly." (In *Rosemont v. Random House*, Howard

Hughes had purchased the copyrights to magazine articles about him, not for the purpose of republishing them, but to prevent writers from using them as a source about him. The court held that a biographer's use of such materials was fair and would not infringe the copyright.)

"But," Latman went on, "where a high school teacher, instead of buying copies, makes his own arrangement and reproduces forty-eight copies for his students, something which is indistinguishable from the situation here, he is held infringing." His example was calculated to catch the attention of Justice Harry Blackmun, who, as a Court of Appeals judge, in a 1962 decision, *Wihtol v. Crow*, joined in a decision that it was not fair use for a choral instructor to make forty-eight copies of a copyrighted song.

If *Wihtol v. Crow* suggested that Justice Blackmun was an ally, so the fact that Justice William O. Douglas was a published author suggested that he might be sympathetic, too. But Arthur Greenbaum, scholarly, almost owlish in his horn-rimmed glasses, was not optimistic. "Mr. Justice Douglas, who at that time was quite ill, was sitting there with his eyes wide open, not blinking, not moving, just sitting there like a wax museum piece. It was very sad." Douglas asked no questions.

Only a few minutes remained in the half hour allotted for his argument, and Latman had so far been able to sidestep the question he feared most. But now Chief Justice Burger returned to the question of Library of Congress practice. "It's not uncommon for judges, members of this Court and others, to call on the Library of Congress for a book, sometimes perhaps it's a book, of which they have only one or a very few copies. At least I assume that, because frequently we get a request, 'Will you please return the book.' Well, sometimes instead of returning the book if we are not finished with it, speaking personally, I have Chapter 13 or Chapter 14 copied on the Xerox machine. As far as I know the Library of Congress has never sent photocopies of anything. They send the original." Is such a borrower, Burger wanted to know, "running up against this statute and these claims by making a copy for his own use, copyrighted material?"

Sitting in the courtroom, Martin Cummings saw this as the turning point. James Davis, too (he had since returned to private practice), wondered, "Oh no, how is he going to handle that one?"

Latman responded, "That is a harder question, which we think is quite different from this case." After circling briefly, he gave his well-prepared answer: "Nobody would sue. And I think that's quite significant here, because it's impractical for anyone to sue."

Charles Lieb, the courtly, white-haired counsel for the Association of American Publishers, who as an *amicus* had submitted a brief in support of Williams & Wilkins, thought: There goes the case! Greenbaum later observed, "We always felt that we could not admit that any kind of copying of a full article was a fair use. Because once you did that, once you admitted that, you were down the slippery slope, and then where did it stop?"

The Chief Justice smiled, deciding not to press the point, deflecting it instead with what in the Supreme Court passes for humor. "Is it your opinion nobody would sue the Chief Justice or that nobody would sue anybody?" The courtroom burst into laughter.

Latman played it straight. "Nobody would sue the Chief Justice or an individual. No one would sue an individual. It's an impractical medium—"

"It's a damage claim," Burger interjected. "Suppose I make

ten copies to send to my colleagues so that we would all be sharing in that. The recovery might be *de minimis*, so that no one would have any incentive to sue."

Latman appeared to have won over the Chief Justice, and now on safe ground, he wove the distinction between institutional and individual copying into the theory of his case. "Exactly. It would be precisely that. And therefore it is to be contrasted with the libraries here which generate, coordinate, install the machinery, decide, incidentally, whether to photocopy or send you the original. They make the decision. They perform the operation, and they have the microfilm camera, they print it themselves, and they give it to you. And the result is some two million pages a year of journal articles being copied by these two libraries alone. So that we can't call it *de minimis*."

Latman could not have hoped to end on a more positive note. After quickly fielding a rhetorical question from Justice Marshall—"You don't want to run the library, do you?"—he ended his argument, reserving a remaining minute for rebuttal.

Robert Bork, wearing the Solicitor General's traditional penguin-like cutaway coat, argued next. The American public knew the Solicitor General's round face, rimmed with wiry gray hair and a wispy fringe of beard, from the publicity that had surrounded his firing of the Watergate special prosecutor, Archibald Cox, in the Saturday Night Massacre a year earlier; thirteen years later he became even better known from the Senate Judiciary Committee hearings on his unsuccessful nomination to the Supreme Court.

Bork's argument for the government was at once brilliant and adventuresome. It was brilliant as a piece of advocacy and as a law school lecture—Bork was on leave from his teaching post at the Yale Law School—illumining corners of public policy that had previously been at best dimly perceived. But it was also adventuresome, bringing the issues to an edge that might compel a decision for Williams & Wilkins. There were smoke and mirrors in the argument, but not all the mirrors reflected back the government's presumably desired result.

With quick precision, Bork spent his opening minutes deftly connecting three lines of analysis into a secure, well-engineered triangle that would enable him throughout the rest of his conversation with the Court to shift easily from one corner of the triangle to another, all the while buttressing the whole. A single, implicit threat coursed through this three-cornered argument: for the Court to hold for Williams & Wilkins, for it to break the triangle, would not only destabilize medical research but undermine all activities requiring access to copyrighted information, without yielding any offsetting benefits for publishers or for society at large.

The first corner of Bork's triangle was an economic argument. Free photocopies do not injure publishers; indeed, they are the most efficient means to put current scientific literature in the hands of researchers. For the second corner, Bork invoked the principle of judicial restraint: if copyright rules are to be changed, it is for Congress, not the Court, to change them. The third argument was at once the most subtle and the most powerful: library photocopying was by now a custom, not just a habit, in which publishers had long acquiesced, and a custom that had taken on the force of law. Publishers and libraries had long agreed to an implicit peace, and it was not for the Court to disturb it.

As evidence of custom and practice, Bork cited the Gentlemen's Agreement. Even if the Agreement looked backward to laborious hand copying and the cumbersome copying technologies of the 1930s, and even if libraries had organized their budgets and operations around assumptions based on these obsolete technologies, these practices were now firmly in place. Bork suggested that Williams & Wilkins was a spoiler. "We are talking here not just about the petitioner. We are talking about five or six hundred publishers of medical journals in very different circumstances. We are talking about thousands of libraries."

Bork underscored that it was not just general custom and practice that Williams & Wilkins was asking the Court to disrupt, but custom and practice in the critically important domain of medical research. Just as Latman had calculated his reference to *Wihtol v. Crow* to get Justice Blackmun's attention, so Bork may have pressed copyright's effects on medical research for the same reason. For nine years in the 1950s, Blackmun had served as in-house counsel for the Mayo Clinic, and the Mayo Foundation had joined with library and other medical groups in filing an *amicus* brief before the Court of Claims in this very case.

Medical research could also be seriously hobbled, Bork now contended, if other publishers were less willing than Williams & Wilkins to enter into blanket licenses. Only United States government libraries enjoy the safe harbor of statutory immunity from injunctive relief. A victory for Williams & Wilkins would enable journal owners to shut down photocopying in other libraries. "I can't imagine the negotiation that would be involved between thousands of libraries and five or six hundred publishers, all with very different interests, very different views of the matter and very different appetites for gain." What we have "is an invitation to chaos," he concluded, "not an invitation to order in the industry."

Bork summarily dismissed Latman's assertion that free photocopies would substitute for paid journal subscriptions. "I suppose, had petitioner taken this trial into the question of how much it was injured, we might have a record on these points. But we have here only petitioner's rather dire speculation about his future, and that's the only record on injury." The message was that if Latman could have proved that library photocopies substituted for journal subscriptions, he would have done so when by law he should have done so—at the trial four years earlier. Bork, still the law professor, could not resist pressing a theoretical point against Latman's factually unproven claim. Drawing on his academic specialty in antitrust law and economics, he advanced an ambitious analogy to the concept of complementary goods. "One looks at these two things and it is apparent in this industry, photocopies of single articles serve a different function and a different market than journal subscriptions. They complement rather than substitute for each other, and therefore I think they are in different markets."

In economists' parlance, a "complementary good" is a product whose price affects the quantity that can be sold of another product, and possibly its price. Pen and ink are complementary goods. Just as a low price for ink will enable pen manufacturers to sell more pens, so, Bork seemed to be arguing, the widespread availability of free photocopies of journal articles will enhance the market for journal subscriptions.

But it was a dangerously flawed analogy. Journal subscriptions and photocopies, though not strictly substitutes, are not strictly complements either. A writer will rarely buy a fountain pen without at some point buying ink. But a researcher will often order a photocopy without buying a subscription. Perhaps sensing this flaw, Bork did not press the point, for that would only have drawn the Court's attention to the truth that the real complementarity lay not between journal articles and photocopies but between journal articles and photocopy machines.

When a library buys or rents a photocopy machine, it is paying for a technical ability to make photocopies. Not surprisingly, it will pay more for the machine if it can make the copies free of any further cost than if it has to pay a license fee each time. (A writer will pay more for a pen that comes with a "free" bottle of ink than he will for one that does not.) Eight years earlier, writing in the Williams & Wilkins house journal, William Passano had put the point in his usual homely terms: "Copyright owners simply want to receive their fair share of the quarter which is put into the slot, or is paid to the individual or the institution which provided the service, or is absorbed by the taxpayers supporting the institution which furnishes photocopies 'for free.' "

Was Solicitor General Bork asking the Court to investigate the proper allocation of consumer payments between the value of the works copied and the value of the machines that made the copies? If the Court were now to hold that library photocopying did not infringe the copyrights in journal articles, would this increase the incentive to invent new forms of copying equipment yet decrease the incentive to produce new literary works? Even in 1974, before videocassette recorders and personal computers had become common household appliances, it was evident that new technologies were dramatically increasing the opportunities to make private copies of copyrighted works. What effect would this decision have on computers and videocassette recorders, and on the software—the computer programs and motion pictures—that they could copy?

Perhaps sensing the hazards of the complementary goods analogy, Bork shifted to the other side of his economic argument. Against the high social cost of negotiations among thousands of publishers and libraries, only a small stream of license fees would flow to publishers. "There are over 400,000 volumes of journals—not individual issues, volumes of journals—in the National Library of Medicine holdings. Now, in 1970 there were 93,000 articles photocopied. That is less than one-fourth of one request per volume of journals held. When you look at this thing spread across the number of journals, sure, there are men microfilming constantly in one library. But when you look at the universe of what they are copying from and see how its impact is negligible upon the individual journals—"

Justice William Rehnquist seemed confused. "In one breath you say the thing is going to result in chaos and then in the next breath you say how negligible it is."

Bork responded, "Yes, that's right, Mr. Justice Rehnquist, and I confess that I think both of those breaths are internally consistent. I'm pointing out that it's negligible as an impact upon an individual journal by showing how thinly it is spread across this vast storehouse of medical information in journals. It is crucial to individual researchers here and there who need a particular article in an obscure, peripheral magazine or in some other magazine or in a back number they have lost or a specialty they don't belong to. For that research it is crucial. The effect at one end upon medical research is quite important. The effect at the other end upon subscriptions to journals is infinitesimal, if it exists. There is no showing in this record that it exists."

Bork buttressed his line of reasoning by returning to another corner of his triangle. If long-standing custom is to be disrupted and economic arrangements reordered, it is for Congress, not the Court, to make that decision. The argument should have struck a responsive chord for at least some of the Justices. The last two times the Supreme Court had addressed a new technological use of copyrighted works, in the *Fortnightly* and *TelePrompTer* cases, it had ruled against liability, holding that cable television systems did not infringe copyright when they retransmitted motion pictures broadcast by local television stations without permission from the copyright owner. In both cases the Court said that the issue was ultimately for Congress to resolve. (Dissenting in *Fortnightly*, Justice Abe Fortas complained, "This case calls not for the judgment of Solomon but for the dexterity of Houdini.")

Greenbaum later observed that *Fortnightly* and *TelePrompTer* "certainly pointed the way, in the sense that here you had cases that were brought too late, and the industries had been created based on doing things in a certain way. And for the Supreme Court to say, 'Well, that's copyright infringement,' would have wiped out the industry. That's what Passano was afraid of. If photocopying went on for another ten years while everybody was talking about it, it would just be too late to do anything about it."

Latman invoked this picture of the future in the one minute he had reserved for rebuttal. "The reason that we are suing in this case is because if this massive system is excused in this case, it's impossible to almost picture what is left of the proprietor's rights. And the important thing, I think, to remember is that we are not just talking about subscriptions as some of the questions, and Mr. Justice Blackmun's question emphasizes. We are talking about all the traditional and new media. The Government and its *amici* conceded that we are talking about a new, separate medium of distribution, and we think that the medium should be encouraged. We don't want to stop it. We want reasonable compensation for it."

After the argument, James Davis went back to his office and wrote a memorandum summarizing the arguments. "My overall reaction is that the Justices were sympathetic to petitioners. They recognized that Bork has a difficult position to defend and I would predict a reversal, recognizing of course that such predictions in the light of oral argument are risky if not foolhardy."

On February 25, 1975, Alan Latman received a telegram informing him of the Court's decision. It consisted of two short sentences:

THE JUDGMENT IS AFFIRMED BY AN EQUALLY DIVIDED COURT.

MR. JUSTICE BLACKMUN TOOK NO PART IN THE DECISION OF THIS CASE.

As it had in the *Gaslight* case, the Court's 4–4 split left the lower court decision standing.

Latman's associate, Carol Simkin, found him in the firm's reception area, telegram in hand. "He was devastated. Not that he had lost. He could have accepted that he lost. But the fact that there was nothing to read. If you lose, at least you get to hear why you lost! You can read what people's analysis was and hear what their response was to your arguments. The fact that after seven years, I think it was seven years, of his full energy, that all he had was this telegram, with one line on it, it just blew his mind."

With no opinion to analyze, no fine points to distinguish one way or the other, Latman and his colleagues fell to playing the inconclusive game of reading the sparse tea leaves of Justice Blackmun's recusal. Had he decided the libraries were right, but declined to vote in their favor because his relationship with the Mayo Clinic might have created an appearance of impropriety? (After the decision, when Cummings telephoned friends at the clinic, one told him that this surely was the case.) Or had Blackmun been persuaded to Williams & Wilkins's point of view and recused himself because, perhaps having encouraged the clinic in the cause, he would now seem disloyal to vote the other way? Not until the Supreme Court's next encounter with fair use, nine years later, would Blackmun make his views on the doctrine known.

"There's something wrong with the legal system that will let that sort of thing happen," Passano wrote in his eulogy for the case, "Journey's End," in the Williams & Wilkins house journal. "Were we given the opportunity to relive the past seven years, we would not have brought our test case against the government libraries, although it seemed so right and proper at the time. In the first place, we were told by the N.L.M. that it would continue to photocopy our journals without our permission until the courts ordered it not to. Furthermore, the library's record of photocopying was readily available from which to select examples on which to build our suit. Most importantly, the N.L.M. is at the very apex of the medical library complex, and where it leads others will likely follow."

Fifteen years later, Passano was at last able to put the case in a larger frame. "Little did I realize at the time that this was all going to have its effect on television and motion pictures and VCRs, and the whole gamut of things which are affected by copyright law, which of course weren't even thought of when we made our move. We were dealing with a fairly simple operation—Xerox. Now it's become horribly complicated."

CHAPTER FOUR

Private Copies

When Chief Justice Warren Burger asked Alan Latman whether a library borrower is running up against the law if he makes a photocopy of a copyrighted text for his personal use, he raised a question at the core of copyright problems today: Do such private copies infringe under the Copyright Act? The Chief Justice understood that massive photocopying by the National Library of Medicine or the National Institutes of Health hardly qualified as private. But what legal principle was there to distinguish library employees' making copies from their simply allowing individual patrons to make the copies themselves? The question of library photocopying put copyright law on a slippery slope, and a decision against the government libraries might one day be used as a precedent to keep an ordinary person from making private copies.

The thought that copyright might be used to control private copies evokes frightening images. Opponents of copyright liability raise the prospect of copyright police invading homes across the country to root out copies made on videocassette machines and audiotape recorders. They also argue that isolated private copying cannot possibly harm the creators of copyrighted works, and cite as evidence that motion pictures, sound recordings, and books continue to be produced despite private copying.

But the question is more complicated than the privacy metaphor would suggest. "Private" copies are made in public as well as private places—a library patron photocopying a short story, a researcher photocopying a journal article in his laboratory, a student photocopying a text in a commercial copy shop. Private copies can also have commercial consequence. As the laborious hand or mechanical copying contemplated by the Gentlemen's Agreement has given way to cheap, fast photocopies, and as newer audio and video technologies have made copying possible where it was impossible before, the risk has grown that "private" copies will displace the retail sales and rentals of the authorized originals from which publishers, record companies, and motion picture producers earn their revenues.

The growing economic importance of private copying is no mirage. In 1983, less than a decade after the *Williams & Wilkins* case, nine percent of the American homes with television also had videocassette recorders; by 1991, the proportion was seventy-one percent. In 1990, the average American household had more than two audiotape recorders capable of making copies. A 1988 survey by the Office of Technology Assessment, the scientific research arm of the United States Congress, found that forty percent of the population age ten or older had taped recorded music during the previous year, a percentage that had roughly doubled in the decade before the survey was done.

Powerful lobbies dominate both sides of this issue. Motion

picture and record companies favor imposing liability on private copying, while consumer electronics manufacturers, such as VCR producers, oppose it. Although these competing pressures have contributed to the stalemate, so, too, have tradition and inertia. Every American copyright act since 1790 has clung to the idea that copyright is a law of public places and commercial interests—retail sales of books, public performances of plays or movies, radio or television broadcasts of every kind of performance. This idea has dominated some of copyright law's central doctrines: only public, not private, performances infringe copyright; noncommercial uses are more likely to be held fair use than commercial ones; to prevail against a fair use defense, a copyright owner must often show that it has suffered economic harm. It is hardly surprising that Congress has chosen not to dismiss the private copy question with Chief Justice Burger's easy attempt at wit: "Is it your opinion that nobody would sue the Chief Justice or that nobody would sue anybody?"

Contributing to the stalemate is the belief that, as a practical matter, private copying cannot be regulated. For example, if Congress were to amend the Copyright Act to prohibit private off-the-air taping of television programs, how would home copiers seek out copyright owners to negotiate a royalty? Even for those willing to pay, the cost of locating and negotiating with the copyright owner would discourage them from even trying. One precept of lawmaking in Washington is that it is bad policy to pass an unenforceable law, for such laws impair fidelity to enforceable laws.

Yet public alternatives to private enforcement do exist. If private conduct cannot be regulated directly, it can sometimes be regulated indirectly. Justice Holmes innovated just such a solution in the *Ben-Hur* case, ruling that the producer of a copyright-infringing motion picture could be held liable for performances of it, even though it was shown by the theater owner and not himself. Similarly, if copyright owners were armed with injunctive and monetary remedies against equipment manufacturers, they could negotiate royalty payments for sales of copying equipment and blank tapes. Until recently, Congress has resisted this solution, possibly because voters may view a tax on home taping media and equipment as impossibly burdensome.

The silence of Congress on the issue of private copies has left a black hole in the center of American copyright legislation. The 1976 Copyright Act categorically gives copyright owners the exclusive right to control reproduction of their works, a right that would literally cover private copying, but the legislative history behind the Act is equivocal. The House and Senate reports on the 1976 Act intimated that tape recording from a broadcast, for example, would not automatically qualify as fair use, yet a 1971 colloquy on the House floor between Abraham Kazen, Jr., a congressman from Texas, and Robert Kastenmeier, chair of the House Intellectual Property subcommittee, suggests the opposite:

MR. KAZEN: Am I correct in assuming that the bill protects copyrighted material that is duplicated for commercial purposes only?

MR. KASTENMEIER: Yes.

MR. KAZEN: In other words, if your child were to record off a program which comes through the air on the radio or television, and then used it for her own personal pleasure, for listening pleasure, this use would not be included under the penalties of this bill?

MR. KASTENMEIER: This is not included in the bill. I am glad the gentleman raises the point.

In the face of all these contending industry forces and thorny enforcement problems, the response in Congress has been to delay. A popular, if not original, tactic has been to appoint a commission to study the problem, or to assign it to an agency such as the Office of Technology Assessment. Between 1975 and 1978, a National Commission on New Technological Uses of Copyrighted Works asked all the right questions about library photocopying and copyright protection for databases; between 1984 and 1992, the OTA considered the general effect of new information technologies on copyright and, more specifically, problems of home audiotaping and computer software protection.

This reluctance to deal with the private copy issue has led to an unusual degree of congressional deference to a pending judicial decision, particularly a Supreme Court decision. Congress put off the library photocopying issue until *Williams & Wilkins*, and similarly deferred consideration of a bill on home videotaping until the Supreme Court could decide the question. In both cases the Supreme Court was asked only to interpret a 1909 copyright statute that was clearly in its waning years. Since Congress could easily pass a law that would reverse any judicial result, why did it defer to the Court? According to Kastenmeier, who chaired the Intellectual Property subcommittee over the course of the deliberations leading to the 1976 Act, "what the Court tends to do is place the burden on the losing party" of getting Congress "to try to change the state of affairs."

Meanwhile, however, the opposing industry groups do not

bear the effects of delay evenly. By and large, copyright owners suffer and consumer electronics companies benefit any
time Congress postpones a decision on home copying. As time
passes, more and more consumers acquire new copying equipment and, with it, the expectation of free copying. As habits of
free use proliferate, the prospects for dislodging them diminish. Ideal, balanced laws that might have been possible within a
year or two of a new technology's arrival in the marketplace
can, five years later, be politically impossible. According to
Kastenmeier, "if you wait until the problem is mature, the industrial interests that are posed one against another may be so
significant" that it is much harder to override them, thereby
"destroying one party commercially or financially, than it
would be had you anticipated the problem years before."

If Congress has failed to resolve the private copy issue, it is
not for lack of attention. Over the last quarter century it has
addressed copyright's clash with private copying technologies
three separate times—first in revising the 1909 Copyright Act
to deal with library photocopying, next in addressing proposed amendments to the 1976 Act to deal with home videotapes and audiotapes. As the issue bounced between Congress
and the courts, the opposing industry and user groups found
themselves forced to adopt new legislative strategies. They
shifted positions on photocopying with each successive decision in the *Williams & Wilkins* litigation; William Passano
reemerged at a crucial moment to prod a legislative compromise. In the case of home videotaping, a Supreme Court
decision, reached only after much behind-the-scenes maneu-
vering, effectively paralyzed Congress. Home audiotaping
found the two sides virtually giving up on congressional
decisionmaking and cobbling together their own compromise
solution instead.

Private Copies

The question of private copies loomed from the very beginning of the legislative efforts that led to the 1976 Act. Alan Latman had first looked into the private copy question when, as a young lawyer, he was asked by the Copyright Office to write a study on fair use to assist in efforts at revising the 1909 Copyright Act. Noting in his study that "the case law is apparently silent on the point," and that one writer had argued that "private use is completely outside the scope and intent of restriction by copyright," Latman cautioned that such categorical conclusions "can neither be supported nor attacked on the basis of authority."

Latman's study was one of thirty-five scholarly papers commissioned by the Copyright Office beginning in the 1950s to analyze problems that had emerged since passage of the 1909 Act. The copyright bar generally applauded these studies but was not nearly so receptive to the conclusions the Copyright Office drew from them. Barbara Ringer, who worked on them as chief of the Copyright Office's Examining Division, observed, "Practically all of them were criticized by somebody, and some of them were criticized by practically everybody." Register of Copyrights Abraham Kaminstein invited suggestions and revisions from affected industry and user groups.

Of all the Copyright Office proposals, from ones on general standards of copyrightability to duration of copyright, none drew sharper attack than the one on photocopying which suggested that libraries should, for research purposes, be allowed to make individual copies of articles in periodicals and of a "reasonable part" of other publications. Publishers argued that copying on this scale was already *unlawful* and that to permit it now would open the door to unrestricted copying; the librarians answered that it was presently *lawful*, and that the exemption did not go far enough. By 1963 they could agree on only one point: the proposal should be dropped. Register Kaminstein acceded: "As important as it is, library copying is only one aspect of the much larger problem of changing technology, and we feel the statute should deal with it in terms of broad fundamental concepts that can be adapted to future developments."

"Broad fundamental concepts" meant fair use. As evolved by the federal courts, and as the Court of Claims considered it in *Williams & Wilkins*, fair use doctrine asks courts to weigh four factors in determining whether an otherwise infringing use of a copyrighted work should be excused: the purpose of the use (courts favor noncommercial over commercial uses); the nature of the work (copiers can take more from a scholarly work than from a work of fiction); the amount taken (less is better than more); and the effect of the use on sales of the copyrighted work (again, less is better than more).

In deciding whether to rely on section 107 of the new copyright bill—the fair use provision—or section 108, which carved out specific exemptions for library photocopies, the librarians and publishers each had to make a strategic choice on which branch of government they wanted to decide the matter. Would librarians or publishers fare better if Congress left it to the federal courts to apply section 107 case by case? Who would fare better under the detailed code of rules that Congress could lay down in section 108? As the *Williams & Wilkins* case advanced through the courts, and sections 107 and 108 made their erratic way through Congress, the two sides regularly changed their strategies.

Kaminstein chose a middle course between the abstractions of fair use and the concreteness of a photocopying code. He proposed a general fair use provision that gave specific examples of what would qualify: "criticism, comment, news reporting, teaching," and—in a bow to the libraries—"scholarship, or research." But both publishers and librarians attacked this compromise, and again the Register retreated, deciding "with some regret" to reduce the fair use section to its bare bones: "The fair use of a copyrighted work is not an infringement of copyright." Authors, publishers, and librarians would have to trust the courts to strike the balance in their favor.

The copyright revision program advanced intermittently in Congress. The early action was in the House, where Robert Kastenmeier's subcommittee devoted twenty-two days to hearings in 1965 and held more than fifty executive sessions in 1966. Four years later, the bill stalled in the Senate, where the question whether libraries would get a privilege to make single copies for library users suddenly emerged as a major issue. (An early Senate bill had limited the permitted copying to internal library uses such as archival preservation.) But on December 10, 1969, the Senate subcommittee chair, John McClellan, reported out a radically expanded single-copy privilege, allowing libraries to make photocopies at the request of their patrons, including requests made through interlibrary loan. Thomas Brennan, McClellan's counsel, recalled, "Our hand was forced by library groups coming forward with the single-copy amendment." The subcommittee tried to mollify the publishers by withholding this privilege if the library had reason to believe that it was engaging in the "related or concerted reproduction" of the same work, but this did not succeed.

Meanwhile, the Copyright Office was in turmoil. Abraham Kaminstein suffered a heart attack and then a stroke; he retired from the Office in 1971. One leading contender to succeed him was Deputy Register George Cary; another was

Barbara Ringer, who had spent her entire career in the Office, had spearheaded the revision program, and was now Assistant Register. (In the 1965 edition of *Contemporary Authors*, a guide to writers and their works, Ringer puckishly listed her "work in progress" as "drafting a bill for general revision of the copyright law.") Ringer's position on photocopying was characteristically forthright: section 107's flexibility was far preferable to section 108's code-like rigidity.

On August 27, 1971, Librarian of Congress Quincy Mumford gave the Register's post to Cary. Four days later Ringer sued to overturn the appointment on grounds of sex and race discrimination. (Ringer, who is white, charged that her rejection was a reprisal against her advocacy of the rights of black Copyright Office employees.) The court ruled for Ringer, finding that Mumford had failed to follow Copyright Office personnel regulations, but the ruling was made on procedural, not substantive, grounds. A month later—having now presumably followed Office regulations—Mumford reappointed Cary, and the Library of Congress Equal Opportunity Office ruled against Ringer in a separate proceeding.

"Once you take a position like that," Ringer remembers, "then everything changes. So I became an opponent and was cut out of anything in the Office." In May 1972, Ringer left Washington to become director of UNESCO's international copyright operations in Paris; but she returned to the Copyright Office in November 1973 when, having won her appeal from the Equal Opportunity Office ruling (and a subsequent challenge by Mumford), she was finally appointed Register of Copyrights.

During Barbara Ringer's time in Paris, section 107's flexible fair use provisions had been pushed aside and the code-like section 108 had taken its place. What if Ringer had been appointed Register when she first applied for the job in 1971? "I think I would have tried to merge 107 and 108. It wouldn't have been easy because they had taken off in different directions. I was conscious that this was very illogical." Although in Ringer's opinion section 108 was "terrible," she added, "When I came back it was absolutely apparent that it could not be touched with a ten-foot pole."

In February 1972, when Commissioner James Davis handed down his decision in *Williams & Wilkins* that library photocopying was not fair use, the librarians, who at least since the days of the Gentlemen's Agreement had assumed that fair use excused their activities, now had second thoughts about the doctrine's presumed safe harbor. Robert Wedgeworth, who had just become executive director of the American Library Association, recalled that the decision "frightened the hell out of the library community." Section 108 now got renewed attention, though librarians did not entirely give up on section 107.

In April 1973, they succeeded in getting a draft Senate report to endorse the principle of private copying as fair use: "The making of a single copy of an article in a periodical or a short excerpt from a book would normally be regarded as fair use." Arthur Greenbaum (who was carrying Williams & Wilkins's brief in Congress while his partner Alan Latman carried it in the courts) objected to the wording. Subcommittee counsel Brennan assured him, "The Subcommittee has not taken any position on whether the practices of the National Library of Medicine relating to the duplication of copyrighted periodical articles would be a fair use if the pending revision bill is enacted."

When in November 1973 the Court of Claims overturned Commissioner Davis's decision for Williams & Wilkins, it was the publishers' turn to seek refuge in section 108. By spring 1974, they focused their efforts on the bill's proposed prohibition against "systematic reproduction" of copies, according to which libraries could engage only in the "isolated and unrelated" reproduction of single copies. The publishers understood that it would be hard to get the subcommittee to alter the statutory wording after all these years, and tried instead to have a favorable definition of "systematic reproduction" included in the Senate report on the bill.

None of the long line of statutory proposals lacked a pedigree. Publishers, authors, and librarians had been negotiating over an acceptable approach to photocopying even before the Register's 1961 Report. Since 1961, with encouragement from the Copyright Office and the House and Senate subcommittees, they had met in venues scattered across Washington—the Cosmos Club, Dumbarton Oaks, and finally the Wilson Room of the Library of Congress. The sum of all these meetings was that the Wilson Room group could not agree on a definition of "systematic reproduction and distribution"; indeed, the group could not even agree on whether librarians had to pay for it, however that term was defined. "There were no facts on the table," Robert Wedgeworth recalled. "It was all personal opinions, conjecture, anecdotal experience."

In February 1975, when the Supreme Court delivered its two-sentence order in *Williams & Wilkins*, the Court of Claims decision in favor of the government libraries was now the law of the land. The six principal library associations urged Kastenmeier to delete, or at least dilute, section 108's imposition of liability on "systematic" photocopying. And the publishers and authors now proposed that this should mean copying where "the purpose or effect" may be to substitute copies "for subscriptions or sales of copies of the journal"—a new compromise that had a certain honest appeal. The Court of Claims in *Williams & Wilkins* had demolished the publishers' first line of attack—that, on principle and regardless of lost subscriptions, they had rights in the photocopying market. Now they were simply asking Congress to convert their factual claim about lost subscriptions into a statutory test. If their factual claim was correct, they would win under section 108; if wrong, they would lose. Kastenmeier's subcommittee quickly incorporated the proposal into the text of section 108 itself.

Section 108's new prohibition on photocopies "in such aggregate quantities" to substitute for sales or subscriptions was, effectively, an acknowledgment by both sides, and the subcommittee, that for fifteen years they had been talking in a vacuum; "personal opinions, conjecture, anecdotal experience" had failed to—and probably could not—identify the point at which photocopying in fact interferes with journal sales and subscriptions. It left the concrete definition of "aggregate quantities" to another day, and if that definition was going to be made by the courts, it would become an *ad hoc* definition, much like fair use decisions under section 107. But if Congress itself could somehow define the term, the self-enclosed integrity of section 108 would be maintained.

Now another group formed to consider the question. On December 31, 1974, a Presidential order created a National Commission on New Technological Uses of Copyrighted Works and placed the photocopy issue at the top of its agenda. The Commission's fourteen Presidentially appointed members came mainly from the publishing, library, and academic communities. Barbara Ringer was an *ex officio* member, and with her prodding, CONTU offered to assist the House and Senate subcommittees by drafting guidelines for section 108's "aggregate quantities," and it spent the next year doing just that. The discussions were far less acrimonious than they had been in the past, possibly because the Commission's chairman, retired New York Chief Judge Stanley Fuld, had no background in copyright law, much less in the photocopy wars. Robert Wedgeworth, one of CONTU's fourteen members, has recalled, "It would be a mistake to say he just presided because he did more than preside. I remember my old high school orchestra leader. I was a percussionist and he said you know the idea for the percussionist is to be felt and not heard. The judge was like that."

With his Supreme Court defeat just months behind him, William Passano made one last effort at a solution: he would present CONTU with a compromise proposal engineered jointly with his former adversary—the National Library of Medicine. Together with Williams & Wilkins's president, Charles Reville, Passano met for lunch in late summer 1975 with Martin Cummings and his deputy, Harold Schoolman. The outcome of their meeting was a plan that Reville and Schoolman would draft a joint letter to Barbara Ringer outlining a basis for compromise. Although the two were able to agree on several points, the effort ultimately failed, and each sent his own letter explaining his views on "systematic reproduction."

While the two letters did not entirely coincide, they did approach common ground on the number of copies that would be considered "systematic reproduction"—Reville's letter referring to copies from journals for which there is "evidence" of a "reasonable demand," Schoolman's quantifying "reasonable demand" as ten requests for copies of articles in a particular journal in any given year. In preparing its defense in the *Williams & Wilkins* case, NLM had accumulated substantial data on library photocopying, and Schoolman knew that very few journals were in such demand. When Wedgeworth asked him whether the Library could agree to five copies annually as evidence of reasonable demand, he readily assented. A late-night telephone call between Wedgeworth and Ringer sealed the compromise.

In the end, CONTU proposed a set of library photocopying guidelines that centered on a numerical compromise—the "rule of fives": " 'Aggregate quantities' means more than five copies a year of any article published in a particular periodical within five years of the date of the request." Showing a penchant for consistency and round numbers, CONTU added that Congress should review the guidelines not later than five years from the Act's effective date.

In September 1976, the House of Representatives passed the copyright revision bill as amended to include section 108's proviso for aggregate copies. The House–Senate Conference Committee accepted the amendment and included the CONTU guidelines in its Conference Report to guide publishers and libraries in the future. The bill passed both houses of Congress, and President Ford signed the bill into law on October 19, 1976.

Winter or spring 1976 might have seemed an ideal time for the motion picture companies to ask Congress to add some form of liability for home videotaping to the pending bill. Home videocassette recorders had been introduced into the American market only the year before, and the best hope was to get Congress to act before the equipment entered too many homes. But, politically, the timing was poor. Approaching the end of a fifteen-year revision effort, Congress was not going to take on yet another controversial issue that might

143

undermine the fragile compromises already reached. Just weeks before the bill passed, Congress dropped an entire title from the text, fearing that continuing controversy over its provisions would destroy the whole effort.

Although litigating a test case was the logical alternative to pressing for a new law, litigation would be risky. One risk was that of losing, of course, and of establishing an adverse precedent for future judicial or legislative action. Also, litigation could easily consume ten years before all appeals were finished, so that even if they won, the film companies might still face the prospect, with videocassette recorders now a common household appliance, of Congress succumbing to grassroots pressure and reversing the result. Nonetheless, in November 1976, Universal City Studios, joined by Walt Disney Productions, took the gamble and filed a copyright infringement lawsuit against the Sony Corporation of America on their own home ground, in the federal district court in Los Angeles, alleging that, by selling its Betamax videotape recorders, Sony was contributing to copyright infringement of the company's televised motion pictures. Following the logic of Justice Holmes's opinion in the *Ben-Hur* case, Universal argued that, by providing people with the instrument of copyright infringement—videocassette recorders—Sony was just as culpable as if it had made off-the-air copies itself.

By building its case on this theory of contributory infringement, Universal hoped to focus the court's attention away from VCR owners, who were the real, direct infringers. But because the law was unclear on whether a court could find contributory infringement if no direct infringer was before it, it took the precaution of including William Griffiths, a client of Universal's law firm, as a nominal defendant. (Griffiths, an admitted home copier, agreed to be sued on the understanding that no damages would be sought against him.) To complete the link between Sony and Griffiths, the film companies also sued several retailers who sold Betamax recorders, and Sony's advertising agency, Doyle Dane Bernbach.

Contributory infringement doctrine is far better developed under patent law than under copyright law, and Sony turned to patent law for an analogy to support its defense. Under the Patent Act, sales of a device—for example, an infrared camera that can be used in a patented process for detecting structural flaws—will be free from the charge of contributory infringement if it also has a "substantial noninfringing use"—such as taking fine art photographs. Sony argued that although some uses of VCRs might infringe copyright, VCRs were also capable of noninfringing uses—such as copying television programs that are not protected by copyright or whose owners do not care about uncontrolled home copying, or are even delighted by it. (Sony enlisted Fred Rogers, of *Mister Rogers' Neighborhood*, to testify that he had no objection to people taping his program off the air. "I think that it's a real service to families to be able to record such programs and show them at appropriate times.")

Both sides understood that fair use would be central in the case. Betamax owners recorded programs off the air for two reasons: to accumulate libraries of televised motion pictures and to time-shift—to tape a prime-time program to view later in the evening when they came home from night shift work, and, after watching it, erase the tape for repeated use. If the court ruled that both library copying and time-shifting were fair uses, the film studios would lose; if the court found both uses to infringe copyright, the film companies would win, because VCRs would then have very few noninfringing uses; and if the court found that one of these uses was fair and the other not, it would have to determine whether the conduct it excused constituted a "substantial noninfringing use."

The decision to litigate rather than legislate posed another problem. Congress can delicately craft laws that are compromises, and it can fine-tune remedies so that the effects of liability are not overly burdensome on anyone. Judicial decisions, by contrast, are all-or-nothing: one side wins; the other side loses. If Universal and Disney prevailed, they would be entitled to an injunction against Sony; a court believing that a decision favoring the film companies would require it to halt Sony's sales in the United States might want to avoid this draconian result simply by finding that Sony was not an infringer.

The trial stages of *Universal v. Sony* moved quickly. The case came to trial early in 1979 and was decided in October of that year. Judge Warren J. Ferguson rejected every one of Universal's arguments. The Copyright Act's exclusive rights did not extend, he ruled, to private, noncommercial copies, whether made for purposes of time-shifting or made for building a library. Even if the Act did extend this far, fair use would exempt home copying; and even if fair use did not apply, no acceptable theory of contributory infringement could expose VCR producers and sellers to liability. Finally, even if producers and sellers were liable, they would not be subject to injunctive relief, since that would harm the defendants and the public far more than denying it would harm the film companies.

The driving force behind Judge Ferguson's decision was the question of harm. Ferguson ruled that the film studios bore the burden of proving that they were harmed by home

146

taping, and he thought they had failed to do so either in the present or for the future. He noted their continuing and increasing profitability, and their admission that no actual harm to their copyrights had yet occurred; and for the future, he observed that the plaintiffs' case was even more speculative than that made by Williams & Wilkins six years before. Their experts "admitted that they knew neither the year in which the predicted harm would occur nor the number of Betamax purchases which would cause the harm."

Judge Ferguson's decision was not the last word in *Universal v. Sony*, and the studios knew how long it could take for their appeal to be decided. (The Ninth Circuit Court of Appeals was at the time painfully slow in deciding appeals, some taking almost three years from argument to decision.) In 1979, when Judge Ferguson issued his decision, VCR producers had sold 475,000 machines in the United States; three years later they would sell more than 2 million units a year, and four years later more than 4 million.

Perhaps sensing the importance of time, the Ninth Circuit moved with unusual speed, deciding the appeal in October 1981, slightly more than eight months after it heard argument in the case. The decision was a sweeping victory for Universal and Disney, all three judges voting to reverse Judge Ferguson's decision. "We find no Congressional intent to create a blanket home use exception to copyright protection and that home video-recording does not constitute fair use. In addition, the appellees are legally responsible for the infringing activity." On the difficult question of injunctive relief, the court added an innovative suggestion. "When great public injury would result from an injunction," a court could instead award damages or a continuing royalty.

Where the District Court had viewed copyright's cup as

half empty, the Court of Appeals now viewed it as half full. "It is clear that home users assign economic value to their ability to have control over access to copyrighted works. The copyright laws would seem to require that the copyright owner be given the opportunity to exploit this market." With most home copying swept into the copyright net, the court's final decision on contributory infringement was all but inevitable: "Videotape recorders are manufactured, advertised, and sold for the primary purpose of reproducing television programming. Virtually all television programming is copyrighted material. Therefore, videotape recorders are not 'suitable for substantial noninfringing use.' "

Some members of Congress were poised for quick action. Two days after the Court of Appeals decision, Democrat Dennis DeConcini, joined by Republican Alfonse D'Amato, introduced a Senate bill to overturn the decision, and Republicans Stanford Parris and John Duncan introduced identical bills in the House. Although the bills differed slightly, their thrust was the same: making home videotapes off the air would not infringe copyright if the copier did not use the tapes for direct or indirect commercial advantage. For the first time, Congress had the issue of private copies squarely before it.

The motion picture companies responded in force. Working through their trade organization, the Motion Picture Association of America, the studios struck on a compromise strategy: they would give up the chance of obtaining injunctive relief in the courts in return for an amendment to the DeConcini bill that would require equipment and tape manufacturers to pay a statutorily fixed royalty on every VCR and blank videocassette sold. (This echoed the Ninth Circuit's suggestion that, on remand, the trial court could withhold an injunction and award only damages against Sony.) Republican Charles Mathias introduced a Senate bill adopting this royalty approach, and two months later California Democrat Don Edwards introduced a counterpart bill in the House.

Months of intense lobbying followed, the Motion Picture Association on one side and, on the other, the Electronic Industries Association joined by the newly formed Home Recording Rights Coalition. Lobbying slowed only when, in June 1982, the Supreme Court agreed to hear Sony's appeal. Although the copyright owners promised to continue their efforts to get Congress to act, one close observer noted that, "being realists, they understood that a chance to do nothing and blame it on another branch of government would be hard for Congress to resist."

In January 1983, the Supreme Court heard argument in *Sony v. Universal.* (The Supreme Court's practice is to give the name of the appealing party, here Sony, first.) As months passed and the end of the Court's term approached, both sides were wondering what decision would be reached after such protracted deliberations; they could not know that, within days of the oral argument, a debate had broken out among the Justices that persisted past the closing days of the term. Nor could they know until a decade later, when the Library of Congress opened Justice Thurgood Marshall's Court papers to the public, that the majority of Justices who had initially lined up on one side of the case dissolved by the end of the term and a new majority formed on the other side.

It was the question of private copies that triggered the Justices' debate. On January 24, six days after oral argument, Justice John Paul Stevens wrote to Justice Blackmun, who had been designated—in the conference where the Justices discussed the case—to write the majority opinion holding for the film companies, that because the question whether a single copy made for private noncommercial use infringes copyright "was not adequately developed during the argument," and "because I expect to emphasize it in dissent, it occurs to me that it may be helpful to you in the preparation of your opinion—and conceivably might persuade one of your adherents to reconsider the matter before positions have become absolutely firm—for me to put the basic outline of my argument on paper."

Stevens addressed the issue of private copies as a matter of statutory interpretation rather than fair use. "Quite remarkably, in the detailed revision of the entire law, Congress studiously avoided any direct comment on the single-copy-private-use question," Stevens observed, and he himself thought that three important values argued for a statutory exemption of private copying: "(1) the privacy interests implicated whenever the law seeks to control conduct within the home; (2) the principle of fair warning that should counsel hesitation in branding literally millions of persons as lawbreakers; and (3) the economic interest in not imposing a substantial retroactive penalty on an entrepreneur who has successfully developed and marketed a new and useful product, particularly when the evidence as found by the District Court indicates that the copyright holders have not yet suffered any actual harm."

Stevens was also alert to the political implications of a Supreme Court decision favoring the copyright owners. If the Court decided not to impose liability on VCR makers, "Congress can confront the problem in the same way that it has confronted and resolved the whole subject of cable television transmissions of copyrighted works. On the other hand, if we affirm, I am afraid the courts will be required to undertake the responsibility of fashioning a detailed series of remedies that can be much better handled by the legislature."

Stevens's letter went also to Justice Lewis Powell, and it unsettled him. He had voted at Conference to affirm—"in accord with the view I held when *Williams and Wilkins* was here"—but on February 3 he told Blackmun that Stevens's private copy argument was new to him and that he needed to "go back to the 'books.' " Blackmun, possibly sensing a drift away from his position, responded: "It may be that the case will have to be reassigned, but, for now, I would like to let that possibility rest until further work has been done."

After a long hiatus, the "further work" appeared in mid-June in the form of a proposed majority opinion by Justice Blackmun and a proposed dissent by Justice Stevens. Blackmun's draft opinion flatly rejected Stevens's claim that in passing the 1976 Act Congress intended to carve out an exemption for single copies made in the home. To be sure, the statutory proscription against copying literally mentioned only "copies," and not a single "copy," but the House and Senate reports had said that references in the plural included the singular, and the Kastenmeier–Kazen colloquy on private copying of sound recordings did not apply to motion pictures. Moreover, when Congress wanted to carve out an exemption for single copies, it knew how to do so, as it had in section 108 on library photocopying. "These limitations would be wholly superfluous if an entire copy of any work could be made by any person for private use." In short, Blackmun concluded, Congress intended fair use, not a *per se* exemption for private use, to separate permissible from impermissible copying.

Justice Stevens's proposed dissenting opinion undertook a sweeping review of copyright's previous encounters with new technologies—player pianos, photocopiers, cable television, and home audiotaping. "This history reveals a remarkable consistency in the way that two themes have reoccurred. First, the Court has repeatedly declined to extend copyright protection until after Congress has evaluated the new development and enacted amendatory legislation; second, no interested party has ever seriously suggested that a penalty, or any form of statutory liability, should be imposed upon an individual for making a single copy of any copyrighted work for his own private use." Perhaps hoping that he could win over a majority of Justices to his position, Stevens carefully drafted his opinion so that by simply replacing the words "should be reversed" with the words "is reversed" in the last sentence he could turn the draft into a majority opinion. The Blackmun and Stevens drafts sparked a flurry of memos from the other Justices that lasted until the very end of the term.

Justice Brennan had initially voted partially to affirm the Ninth Circuit, drawing a distinction between videotape library building, which infringed, and time-shifting, which did not. Now he said he would vote to reverse entirely. Rejecting Stevens's position that Congress had categorically exempted private copying from liability, he proposed a subtle but crucial shift in the test for contributory infringement. Instead of looking at the VCR's "primary use" as the basis for contributory infringement, he would ask only whether "the Betamax has substantial noninfringing use," and, if it did, he would find no contributory infringement. Most time-shifting, in Brennan's view, qualified as such a noninfringing use.

Three days later, Justice Byron White weighed in. Although he inclined to Stevens's position on an exemption for private copies, he agreed with Brennan that Sony was not a contributory infringer. "John, of course, would reverse the judgment against Sony for his own reasons, but can't you two get together?" After all, he said, "if there were five votes to reverse as to Sony, the issue of the homeowner is hardly a pressing question," because "no relief was sought against the homeowner." Stevens responded immediately to Brennan's lead on contributory infringement. "If there are five votes for that approach, I will be more than happy to recast my memorandum into an opinion taking that position."

At the same time that Brennan and White were moving toward reversal on the contributory infringement ground, Justice Sandra Day O'Connor was moving toward reversal on the more intricate question of harm. "I have considerable difficulty in rejecting the District Court's view that the respondents suffered no harm, actual or potential, as a result of Sony's use," she wrote to Blackmun. Blackmun replied that he thought the District Court's opinion was less conclusive than she did on the question of potential harm, but, he asked, "In light of our differing readings of the opinion, what would you think of remanding to the District Court for further consideration of the issue of harm?" O'Connor declined this offer. "It appears clear that whatever standard we ask the District Court to apply, the result is very likely to be the same given the court's strongly expressed view that the harm in this case was entirely too speculative to establish even 'probable' harm." Anyway, as a matter of law, she thought the copyright owner should bear the burden of proof about harm. "The burden of proof on harm and damages traditionally remains with the plaintiff, and I see no sufficient reason to shift it to the alleged infringer."

True to his reputation as a consensus builder, Justice Brennan wrote to Blackmun the same day. "The suggestions Sandra has made to you in this difficult case seem very

constructive, and I shall be most interested in your response."
Two days later, Powell wrote in the same vein: "The suggestions made in Sandra's letter of June 18 appeal to me," and "if
you should revise your opinion generally along the lines of
her letter, I believe I could join you. As the case was assigned
to you—in part I suppose—on the basis of my Conference
vote, I feel some obligation to remain with you absent a gen-
uine conviction to the contrary."

On June 20, Blackmun wrote to his so far unswerving supporters, Thurgood Marshall and William Rehnquist, that he
was willing to try to accommodate O'Connor, Powell, "and,
possibly Bill Brennan," adding, "I do not wish to undermine
your support." He was willing to retreat on the issue of
harm—"I do not think it would be unreasonable to require
the copyright owner to show a potential for harm"—and on
the standard for contributory infringement—"I agree that the
question of contributory infringement turns on the amount
of VCR use that is infringing rather than the amount of television programming that is copyrighted."

O'Connor now pressed her evolving view on a copyright
owner's obligation to prove harm, this time proposing specific
wording to be included in Blackmun's opinion. By June 28,
an evidently exasperated Blackmun gave up on his efforts to
accommodate her views. "My letter of June 23 to you represents the limit of what I am willing to do. Five votes are not
that important to me when I feel that proper legal principles
are involved. It therefore looks as though you and I are in
substantial disagreement. The case will have to go its own way
by a different route from the one I have proposed." Clearly,
Blackmun's majority had eroded.

On June 27, Brennan told the other Justices that Stevens's
draft "comes closer to expressing the views I expressed at

Conference and in my memorandum of June 14." A day later, having received Blackmun's final letter, O'Connor wrote to Chief Justice Burger that there had been "many late nights, and much redrafting. The result has been a decided shift to a 'middle' position on the merits and a movement toward a more restrictive stance on contributory infringement." Noting that Blackmun had refused to make any further changes in his approach, she added, "I am closer to John's most recent draft than to any other now 'on the table.' "

It was becoming increasingly evident to all the Justices that, although a new majority position had emerged, the press of other cases right at the very end of the term would make it hard to craft a majority opinion in so short a time. Putting the case down for reargument the next year was a temporizing solution. In a "Dear Chief" letter, Stevens told Burger on June 28 that he had "sent to the Printer a revised draft of my memorandum in which I have tried to reflect what I understand to be a consensus of views that are shared by you, Bill Brennan, Byron, Lewis, Sandra and myself. The memorandum is in a form that could be converted into an opinion if there are five votes to support it. If that should happen, I would hope that it would not be necessary to reargue the case."

It did not happen. The Justices had simply run out of time. On July 6, the Court restored the case to its calendar for reargument during the next term.

Thurgood Marshall, along with Rehnquist, Blackmun's only unwavering source of support, had throughout the spring confined his memos to a cheering one or two lines—"Go to it. I will more than likely still be with you." "I am still with you." But on October 4, 1983, the day after the parties reargued *Sony*, Marshall weighed in with a seven-page analysis of the harm caused by time-shifting. Viewing copyright's cup as half full, not half empty, he suggested that time-shifters themselves formed a potential market for copyrighted programs. "Those people are willing to pay for the privilege of watching copyrighted works at their convenience, as evidenced by the fact that they are willing to pay for VCRs and tapes; undoubtedly, most would also be willing to pay some kind of royalty to the copyright holders."

Blackmun replied two days later that he thought that Marshall's points were sound. "I shall endeavor to incorporate them into the forthcoming dissent." Between Marshall's memo and Blackmun's response, the Justices had held their conference, voting mainly along the lines that had emerged at the end of the previous term. The final tally, as announced in the Court's January 17 decision: Brennan, Burger, O'Connor, Stevens, and White to reverse the Ninth Circuit; Blackmun, Marshall, Powell, and Rehnquist to affirm.

Justice Stevens's opinion for the majority resembled the Brennan and O'Connor memos of the previous term more than it did his original dissent. The opinion made no mention of a statutory exemption for private copying. Contributory infringement would be found only if the product in issue had no substantial noninfringing use. Time-shifting was a noninfringing use—in part because many copyright owners like Fred Rogers would happily consent to it, in part because it constituted fair use. If the private, noncommercial nature of time-shifting did not categorically exempt it from copyright infringement, it at least created a presumption, unrebutted by Universal or Disney, that they had not been harmed.

Justice Blackmun's dissent closely followed his original proposed majority opinion from the previous term. The main additions were Justice Marshall's point on potential markets, copied almost verbatim, and a harsh rebuttal of Justice

Stevens's historical assessment of the proper relationship between the Court and Congress in the face of technological change: "Perhaps a better and more accurate description is that the Court has tended to evade the hard issues when they arise in the area of copyright law. I see no reason for the Court to be particularly pleased with this tradition or to continue it. Indeed, it is fairly clear from the legislative history of the 1976 Act that Congress meant to change the old pattern and enact a statute that would cover new technologies, as well as old."

The last hope for the film companies now was Congress. Optimistic members of the industry could take heart from Justice Stevens's observation that Congress had in the past regularly filled the void when the Supreme Court ruled against copyright liability—from its extension of rights against pianola rolls and phono records after the Court's *Apollo* decision, through its legislation on cable television and library photocopying. But none of these cases or statutory measures directly involved the bedeviling question of private copies. By the time the Court decided *Sony v. Universal*, the number of American homes with VCRs had jumped from almost zero, when the case was filed, to nine percent. When Congress declined to act on S.31, the compromise measure imposing a statutory royalty on recording equipment and blank tapes, the motion picture companies were not inclined to press the point. Home videotaping disappeared as a serious issue on the legislative agenda.

The film companies' setbacks in the Supreme Court and in Congress put the record companies in a quandary. They had succeeded in annexing an audiotape levy to the film companies' proposed videotape levy in S.31, and their hopes for a quick legislative solution to the private copy problem ended with the bill's demise. *Sony v. Universal* offered at best conflicting signals about their chances for ultimate success in litigation. The decision dealt only with videotapes and gave no clue as to how the Court would view home audiotaping. The record companies knew that consumers usually make off-the-air audiotapes to assemble musical libraries, not to time-shift, but they had to be troubled lest a court use the Kastenmeier–Kazen colloquy about home audiotaping as evidence that Congress intended to exempt home audiotaping from copyright liability.

Two years after *Sony v. Universal*, a new technology was launched on the market that both heightened the record companies' concerns and ignited a short fuse for congressional action. In 1986, the consumer electronics industry introduced a new product, the digital audiotape recorder, a product developed and manufactured not in the United States but overseas. Digital audiotape offered more than just the crystalline sound quality of digital compact discs. It also gave home users a feature that CDs did not: the ability to make copies. From the consumer's viewpoint, the advantage was that, unlike analog tapes, whose sound quality deteriorates with each successive copy, digital tapes promised not only flawless reproductions from original tapes but equally flawless copies of copies. For record companies, the proliferation of unending generations of flawless copies spelled doom for the retail sales market.

Digital audiotape recorders, it was believed, would become the home taping device of choice, displacing the widespread but technically inferior analog recorders. If the record companies could temporarily hold off the importation of digital tape equipment by threat of lawsuits, and at the same time move quickly in Congress, they might well succeed in winning some measure of copyright control over the new technology before it became so entrenched in the American marketplace that congressional action would be impossible.

As a first step, the Recording Industry Association of America threatened to sue digital audiotape recorder manufacturers on a contributory infringement theory similar to the one that Universal and Disney had used against Sony. The tactic was risky, for any manufacturer could take up the challenge and win a decision that private copies do not infringe copyright. But the equipment manufacturers had equal reason to fear litigation: whatever the outcome, it could tie up their products in the courts for years. Also, the manufacturers knew that without the record industry's cooperation they would have no songs to put on their prerecorded digital cassettes—an essential requirement if they were to get people to buy their machines. For the moment, no home machines were imported and no lawsuit was filed.

Meanwhile, the record companies planned a noncopyright strategy: they would seek the mandatory incorporation in prerecorded digital tapes of a signal that would defeat the making of copies. But even a technological fix like this was not without risk. At the *Betamax* trial, when Universal sought to put on an expert witnesses to testify about the availability of a low-cost jamming device that would make it impossible to record a television program without the copyright owner's permission, Judge Ferguson observed that if he ordered Sony to put such a device in its machines, "as sure as you or I are sitting in this courtroom today, some bright young entrepreneur, unconnected with Sony, is going to come up with a device to unjam the jam. And then we have a device to jam the unjamming of the jam and we all end up like jelly."

Still, in early 1987, bills were introduced in the House and

Senate that required the incorporation of a copyguard system in any digital studio recording equipment sold in the United States. Hearings centered on the Copycode system, developed by CBS Records, in which a signal embedded in a pre-recorded tape indicates that the recording is protected by copyright; on detecting the signal, a chip installed in the recording device prevents the making of a copy. Would this untried technology be effective? The subcommittees asked the National Bureau of Standards to test it; the Bureau reported back that the system impaired sound quality and in some cases also prevented the recording of *un*copyrighted material, and the bills were dropped.

Time was now working against the record companies. In spring 1987, Congress had asked the Office of Technology Assessment to look at home audio copying with the same cold eye it gives to questions such as airport congestion and the accuracy of lie detectors. It was believed that the study (with its advisory committee chaired by a senior fellow in the Economic Studies Program at the Brookings Institution) might well challenge the claim that the record industry suffers economic harm from home taping, for drafts, circulating since 1988, were not sympathetic to the record industry's claims. In the end, although the report found an increase in the incidence of home audiotaping, it also acknowledged that the factual assessment of home taping's effect on sales of prerecorded music was far from clear.

By mid-1989, while the OTA report was in press, record company and consumer electronic company representatives, meeting in Athens, Greece, announced they had reached a compromise, to be implemented by national legislation, on digital audiotape recording. It centered on a new technological fix, the Serial Copy Management System, which, when incorporated in a digital tape recorder, would allow the machine to copy an original prerecorded cassette—so that any original prerecorded work could be copied endlessly—but would block the machine from making a copy of a copy. The Athens agreement committed the parties to seeking government implementation of an SCMS standard around the world. For the American record companies, this compromise would help them avoid the legislative delays that had slowed resolution of the library photocopying issue and had sunk the videotape and audiotape levy bills. For the equipment manufacturers, it would enable them to enter the American marketplace quickly, and with an abundance of prerecorded tapes. However, the strategy suffered a major defect: it failed to include the interests of composers and music publishers.

When, in June 1990, Senator Dennis DeConcini chaired hearings on a bill requiring the installation of SCMS in digital tape recordings, songwriters and music publisher representatives testified in opposition. Home taping would cut into their revenues, they argued, and because the bill had no provision for a statutory royalty, these losses would go uncompensated. While they were making their case to Congress, Sony began to import digital tape recorders into the United States, and this new coalition filed a suit against them, alleging that Sony's importation contributorily infringed their copyrights. DeConcini made it clear that his bill would not go forward until the music interests had been accommodated.

The equipment manufacturers now faced a hard strategic choice. They could reject a statutory royalty and see the Athens agreement dissolve—and, with it, the prospect for quick entry into the American market; or they could accept a statutory royalty and, with it, a principle—payment of a levy on their products—they had resisted since the advent of

VCRs. In congressional lawmaking, where precedent can weigh as heavily as it does in judicial lawmaking, a concession on digital tape or equipment levies might lead to levies on still other copying media, new and old, levies that would only increase prices on the companies' products and decrease sales.

John Roach, chairman and CEO of Tandy Corporation, took up the negotiating lead for the equipment producers and, together with the Recording Industry Association and the National Music Publishers' Association, hammered out an agreement in principle and encouraged their constituents to sign on. Industry lawyers then turned to the arduous task of drafting a detailed statutory proposal that would be acceptable to everyone. Once the parties reached agreement, the composers and publishers dropped their lawsuit against Sony.

As finally passed by Congress and signed into law by President George Bush in October 1992, the Audio Home Recording Act of 1992 required not only the incorporation of SCMS controls in digital audio equipment sold in the United States, but also a statutory levy to be paid by the producers of blank digital audiotapes and digital audiotape equipment—three percent of the sales price in the case of tapes, two percent in the case of equipment. Once deposited in the Copyright Office, the levies would be divided into two funds to be distributed annually, two-thirds to the Sound Recordings Fund, and one-third to the Musical Works Fund. So, for example, in the case of each nine-dollar blank tape, the Sound Recordings Fund would receive eighteen cents and the Musical Works Fund would receive nine cents. After four percent was taken off the top of the Sound Recordings Fund (less than a penny per nine-dollar tape), to be divided between the background musicians and vocalists on the recording, the remainder of the eighteen cents would be distributed sixty percent to the record companies and forty percent to featured recording artists; publishers and writers would share 50–50 in the Musical Works Fund, each receiving 4.5 cents for every cassette.

In return for these royalties and for the SCMS, copyright owners gave up all but the most slender thread of their claim against private audio recording. Under the terms of the Act, a consumer is free to copy a prerecorded cassette—digital *or* analog—for private noncommercial use, such as in an automobile cassette player. However, the Act doesn't say that this private copy is not an infringement of copyright—only that "no action may be brought under this title alleging infringement of copyright." The distinction between an exemption from infringement and a prohibition against suing for infringement is a fine, possibly invisible, one. But for copyright owners, the distinction has a powerful symbolic effect, at least preserving the illusion that private copies may in fact infringe copyright, and forestalling a precedent for future efforts to obtain an exemption for home copies.

This kind of solution was new to the United States, but levies of this kind had been a feature of European copyright law since the Federal Republic of Germany's enactment in 1965 of a statute providing compensation to copyright owners for the private copying of their works. Several European countries have enacted a "public lending right"—Denmark adopted the first in 1946—to compensate writers for the potential income they lose when library patrons borrow rather than purchase their books. After a long and bitter fight between authors and librarians, the United Kingdom adopted such a right in 1979. The English system uses computerized sampling techniques to determine how many times each book is borrowed and rewards the author accordingly; by

1984, a British author received 1.02 pence each time his book was borrowed.

Would this new congruence of American and European systems promise American copyright industries a share in the increasingly rich European market? Or would centuries-old divisions between these two cultures of copyright stand in the way? The question moved toward the top of America's agenda for international trade. And the slowly dawning answer has been an unsettling surprise.

The Two Cultures
of Copyright

In March 1986, the media entrepreneur Ted Turner purchased Metro-Goldwyn-Mayer, a once powerful but now money-losing film studio, from the financier Kirk Kerkorian for $1.6 billion. Within three months, Turner returned to Kerkorian MGM's production and distribution operations as well as its famous roaring lion logo, and sold off the studio's film laboratory and real estate. The series of transactions left Turner with a $1.1 billion investment in a single asset—MGM's film library of more than 3,600 motion pictures, including such classics as *Casablanca*, *Gone with the Wind*, and *The Wizard of Oz*. Now Turner—not the writers or producers or directors, let alone MGM—controlled the copyrights in all those movies.

Turner knew that engineers had recently developed a computer-assisted technique for turning black-and-white films into vivid—some critics said too vivid—color, and he appreciated that this colorization could breathe new economic life into the many black-and-white films in MGM's library. The idea was that television viewers would switch channels if a black-and-white movie came on the screen but would stay to watch a colorized version. Turner's decision to colorize one of the films in the MGM library, John Huston's *The Asphalt Jungle,* and to license the French television channel La Cinq to broadcast it, put him on a collision course with copyright law in France, where the underlying view about the rights of film directors, writers, and other artists differs dramatically from that prevalent in the United States.

French copyright law sanctifies the rights of the author— be it of a text, a piece of music, a film, or any other original work. The French doctrine of moral right—*droit moral*—entitles authors to maintain control over what they create, and to keep anyone, even their own publishers, from changing their works in any way that might affect their artistic reputation. In the words of one French scholar, the moral right affirmed in French copyright law aims at securing "the intimate bond that exists between a literary or artistic work and its author's personality." When a French department store changed some of the images in a painting by Henri Rousseau that was reproduced for use in a window display, the painter's granddaughter won a lawsuit against the store. Other European nations—indeed, much of the rest of the world—each in its own way takes the same position, deriving as it does from precepts of civil law that are followed in many countries.

The U.S. Congress has steadfastly resisted efforts to import the doctrine of moral right into American copyright law. When Congressman Richard Gephardt introduced a bill in 1987 to prohibit the unauthorized alteration of motion pictures, including their colorization, most observers correctly predicted that the bill would not pass. In 1989, in the United States at least, Ted Turner could say, "I think the movies look better in color, pal, and they're my movies."

With scant prospects for success in the United States, John Huston's heirs, joined by the film's screenwriter, Ben Maddow, filed suit against La Cinq in Paris, asserting that the station's broadcast of the colorized version of *The Asphalt Jungle* would violate Huston's and Maddow's moral rights. Before the French court could address their claim, it first had to decide what body of law governed the performance of an American-made film in France.

Under "choice of law" rules, a court may choose to decide a case, not according to the law of the country or state which it sits in, but according to the law of some other jurisdiction. If a New Jersey plumbing supply company makes a contract to deliver goods to a purchaser in Wyoming, but the purchaser refuses to accept delivery, the Wyoming court where the supplier files suit would have to determine whether to use New Jersey law or Wyoming law in deciding the case. Similarly, when Maddow and the Huston heirs filed suit in Paris, the court there had to determine whether the law governing the dispute was that of the United States, where Huston and Maddow had signed their contracts and made the film, or that of France, where the colorized version of the film was to be broadcast.

Maddow and the Huston heirs handily won the initial rounds of their lawsuit in the French trial and appellate courts. But on July 6, 1989, in a critical phase of the case, the Paris Court of Appeals ruled for Turner and La Cinq, holding that American law, not French law, controlled the arrangement between Huston, Maddow, and the film studio that had employed them. A unique doctrine of United States copyright law governed this arrangement. Under the "work for hire" doctrine, the studio, having employed Huston and Maddow to make the film, was not only the film's copyright owner but also its very author; any moral rights that an author might have belonged not to Huston and Maddow but to the film studio. And Turner had obtained the film studio's rights.

This decision shocked most observers, who had long believed that the governing law on issues of authorship is the law of the country where the infringement occurs—in this case, France, where the colorized film was to be broadcast. Few were surprised, then, when the French high court, the Court of Cassation, reversed the Paris Court of Appeal. French law governed the ownership of rights in *The Asphalt Jungle*, it ruled, including the authors' moral rights. Since under French law only real flesh-and-blood people like Huston and Maddow, not corporate entities like a film studio, can qualify as authors, it was they, and not the film studio, who were the authors of the film.

Commentators regularly cite the doctrine of an author's moral right, and its rejection in the United States, as evidence of a profound and pervasive division separating two cultures of copyright—the European copyright culture, shared with other countries following the continental civil law tradition, and the American copyright culture, shared with countries belonging to the English common law tradition. The European culture of copyright places authors at its center, giving them as a matter of natural right control over every use of their works that may affect their interests. (Indeed, many European countries call their statutes protecting literary and artistic works, not "copyright" laws at all, but "author's rights" laws—*droit d'auteur* in France, *Urheberrecht* in Germany, *diritto d'autore* in Italy.) By contrast, the American culture of copyright centers on a hard, utilitarian calculus that balances the needs of copyright producers against the needs of copyright consumers, a calculus that appears to leave authors at the margins of its equation.

According to the accepted wisdom, this divide between the two cultures of copyright has consequence not only philosophically but also in the economic sphere, in the marketplace where literary and artistic works are bought and sold. This view holds that European lawmakers are perennial copyright optimists, who consistently treat copyright's cup as half full and, to protect authors' interests, will extend rights into every corner that might have economic value. American lawmakers, by contrast, are viewed as chronic copyright pessimists, who see copyright's cup as half empty and do not extend rights against new uses of copyrighted works unless copyright owners can show they need them as an incentive to continue producing literary and artistic works.

Precedent offers some support for this accepted view of the situation. When in *Sony v. Universal* the U.S. Supreme Court refused to apply the Copyright Act's flat command, "Thou shalt not copy," to the private copying of televised motion pictures, it based its refusal on a finding that the film companies had not shown that uncontrolled private copying would reduce their incentive to produce motion pictures. But thirty years earlier, when West Germany's Supreme Court faced a similar case, it ruled for the copyright owners, following the natural rights precept that, when in doubt about a statute's meaning, the statute should be construed in favor of the copyright owner. Acknowledging that the German Copyright Act, passed in 1901, exempts handwritten copies made for private use, the court concluded that the law could not have contemplated mechanical recording devices; given a choice between reading the private use exemption narrowly or broadly, the court tipped the balance in the copyright owners' favor and found infringement.

Just as moral right is the preeminent symbol of the author's rights culture, fair use, the doctrine at the heart of the *Sony* case, symbolizes the more pragmatic American culture. Fair use is a hard-edged economic instrument that will excuse an unauthorized use of a copyrighted work as being a fair one any time it is too costly for the parties to negotiate a license. In the great majority of cases where courts have upheld a fair use defense—cases such as *Sony* and *Williams & Wilkins*—the cost of negotiating for the home videotaping or library photocopying exceeded the economic value of the use to which the copy was put, making it unlikely that the copier would have tried to negotiate a license. Fair use operates on the pragmatic notion that half a loaf is better than none: without it, the copyright owner would get no revenues because the costs of negotiating a license are insuperably high, while the prospective user would for the same reason get no copy; with it, the copyright owner still gets nothing, but the user at least gets to make a copy.

But in fact, putting the emblems of moral right and fair use to the side, the two cultures of copyright have much in common. The similarities lie not only in the practicalities of the marketplace but in the laws' underlying premises. This convergence has more than academic significance, for the notion of two diverging cultures of copyright has made for unnecessary obstacles in international transactions, as Ted Turner discovered in Paris; more significantly, it has been used to rationalize governments' protectionist postures in international copyright trade.

The historical foundations of French copyright law are remarkably similar to those of American copyright law. As in England, copyright in France emerged out of the disintegration of royal monopolies and state literary censorship. For close to a century, copyright law in France was torn by the same question that early occupied courts in England and the United States in *Millar v. Taylor*, *Donaldson v. Becket*, and *Wheaton v. Peters*: Is copyright a natural right of the author that lasts in perpetuity, or is it a more limited instrument of public policy aimed at encouraging literary and artistic production? Throughout the debate, French publishers and printers, like the Stationers in England, waged battle under the authors' banner.

The French copyright scholar Pierre Recht has observed, "When *droit moral* fanatics discuss moral rights, they take the attitude of a religious zealot talking of sacred things or of a Girondin reading the Declaration of the Rights of Man." The most ardent advocates of the author's rights tradition trace the doctrine back to the Middle Ages; more moderate scholars, to the spirit of individual rights that permeated the French Revolution. But as Jane Ginsburg of Columbia Law School has demonstrated in a pathbreaking study, author-centered copyright emerged in France only gradually over the course of the nineteenth century. Before that, French courts regularly balanced the needs of copyright users against the interests of copyright owners and, like their American counterparts, early ruled that failure to comply with formalities—deposit of two copies with the Bibliothèque Nationale—forfeited an author's right to sue for copyright infringement.

The influence of these old attitudes persists in contemporary French doctrine. In France, copyright lasts for a prescribed period, not perpetuity: seventy years after the author's death. (Only moral rights are considered to be perpetual.)

Also, just as fair use doctrine in the United States has exempted private uses of copyrighted material, the French copyright act exempts "copies or reproductions reserved strictly for the private use of the copier"—whether this private copy is made by hand or by a mechanical device such as a photocopier. And the French statute, like American fair use doctrine, may excuse parodies from copyright liability.

Just as French and other author's rights laws are less sweeping than the boundless logic of natural rights would suggest or require, the U.S. Congress has been far more consistent in extending rights against economically valuable uses than a strict showing of needed incentives would appear to indicate. Measured by the political standard of "Watch what I do, not what I say," it has, for a century, generally treated copyright's cup as half full, not half empty—from the grant of rights against unauthorized translations and dramatizations in 1870 to the 1992 Home Recording Act. Representatives and senators may regularly invoke the principle that copyright owners bear the burden of persuading Congress of the need to bring new rights within the sweep of copyright, but Congress has never once required authors or publishers to demonstrate that, in fact, they need the new right as an incentive to produce literary and artistic works.

When toward the end of the nineteenth century, Europe began to extend copyright's reach, author's rights became the rallying cry and natural rights the rationale. American lawmakers never picked this up, but they did not lack a theoretical underpinning for their contemporaneous expansion of copyright. The same utilitarianism that had governed American copyright in the past gave them the rationale, this time coupled with an intuition that, as markets for copyrighted works expanded, a balanced system of incentives required copyright, too, to extend to these new markets. This first became explicit only a century later, in the 1970s, when the so-called law and economics movement in American universities first shed the searching light of "welfare economics" on the workings of the copyright system. This school of thought measures the desirability of a particular legal rule against the criterion of consumer welfare. A law—such as antitrust law, say—is good if, by promoting competition, it ensures that consumers get the widest variety of goods at the lowest possible price. Copyright law was a natural candidate for this mode of economic analysis.

Both optimists and pessimists about copyright can be found among the economists who wrote on this subject, beginning with Adam Smith in the late eighteenth century. Smith rejected the idea of writers' having an unfettered natural right to their published works, but nonetheless believed that some limited form of statutory protection was justified "as an encouragement to the labours of learned men." He understood that copyright was a monopoly, not in the baleful sense of a businessman's cartel, such as the Stationers' Company, bent on controlling book production and driving up prices, but as a highly constrained property right that exposed the works it protected to competition with other works in the marketplace. Copyrights thus stood apart from institutional or industry-wide monopolies. "As they can do no harm and may do some good," he wrote, they "are not to be altogether condemned."

Adam Smith's lukewarm endorsement hardly amounted to a full-scale rationale for copyright. And he left many questions unanswered. What did he mean when he said that copyright does "no harm" and "may do some good"? Was it that the public is getting something—a new book of poems, or a gazetteer—that it would not have had otherwise? What evidence was there that writers and publishers needed copyright to encourage the required labor and investment? Was there any reason to believe that a twenty-eight-year term of copyright, neither more nor less, was the correct incentive?

Jeremy Bentham took up the task of making an affirmative case for copyright. He focused on the question of incentives, on whether, without copyright, writers would write and publishers publish. Starting from the observation "that which one man has invented, all the world can imitate," he concluded that in a competitive marketplace only laws can deter such imitation, and that, otherwise, creative individuals would find themselves driven out of the market by rivals who, "without any expense, in possession of a discovery which has cost the inventor much time and expense, would be able to deprive him of all his *deserved* advantages, by selling at a lower price." In short, "he who has no hope that he shall reap, will not take the trouble to sow."

The great essayist, politician, and historian Thomas Babington Macaulay accepted Bentham's point about the need for incentives, but he challenged Bentham's—and Smith's—evident assumption that copyright did little or no harm. The occasion for Macaulay's observations was an 1841 House of Commons debate on the nagging question of the proper length of the copyright term. (From the time of the first English copyright act, publishers had continued to press for longer ones.) The Commons was considering whether to extend the term from twenty-eight years to one that, like the French law, would end at a prescribed period—sixty years after the author's death.

Macaulay opposed this, but he started with a debater's ploy, painting the positive case for copyright. "It is desirable that we should have a supply of good books," he began, and copyright is far more reliable than royal or aristocratic patronage in ensuring that supply. "We cannot have such a supply unless men of letters are liberally remunerated; and the least objectionable way of remunerating them is by means of copyright." But, Macaulay added, monopoly is an evil; it is "a tax on readers for the purpose of giving a bounty to writers." Consequently, and here was the pivot of his argument, "the evil ought not to last a day longer than is necessary for the purpose of securing the good."

Macaulay cited the example of Samuel Johnson. "Dr. Johnson died fifty-six years ago. If the law were what my honourable and learned friend wishes to make it, somebody would now have the monopoly of Dr. Johnson's works." But, Macaulay asked, "would the knowledge that this copyright would exist in 1841 have been a source of gratification to Johnson? Would it have stimulated his exertions? Would it have once drawn him out of his bed before noon?" While the added incentive to Johnson would have been small, the added cost to readers would have been high. "Considered as a reward to him, the difference between a twenty years' term and sixty years' term of posthumous copyright would have been nothing or next to nothing. But is the difference nothing to us? I can buy *Rasselas* for sixpence; I might have had to give five shillings for it . . . Do I grudge this to a man like Dr. Johnson? Not at all . . . But what I do complain of is that my circumstances are to be worse, and Johnson's none the better; that I am to give five pounds for what to him was not worth a farthing."

Macaulay's insight about copyright's drawbacks applied not only to the duration of a copyright term—the House of Commons voted down the proposed extension—but also to copyright's scope. What uses of a given text should copyright be allowed to control? Should the "evil" of copyright extend to uses whose control was more than was "necessary for securing the good"? A reader can read a book or copy a passage from it without stopping anyone else from reading or copying the same work, just as a student can get a photocopy of a scholarly article without stopping another researcher from photocopying or reading it. One reader or one million can simultaneously read a novel without interfering with its enjoyment by anyone else. Compare this to an apple: one person's devouring the apple will make it impossible for anyone else to eat it.

This unique characteristic of the goods with which copyright is concerned—that anyone can "use" them without diminishing their availability to anyone else—gives rise to a powerful moral and economic argument. Since copyright allows creators and publishers of literary and artistic works to charge a price for gaining access to these works, the inescapable effect is to withhold the work from people who will not or cannot pay that price, even though giving them free access would harm no one else. But—and here is the great dilemma of copyright—to withhold copyright may be equally harmful: "He who has no hope that he shall reap, will not take the trouble to sow."

It remained for Kenneth Arrow (who later won the Nobel Prize in Economic Science) to bring the moral and practical intuitions of Smith, Bentham, and Macaulay to hard economic ground in an essay published in 1962. Like Bentham, he observed that creative individuals, and the business enterprises to which they entrust the dissemination of their works, will not sow where they cannot reap; to this he added the economist's point that free markets have no effective mechanism for getting users to join together to share in the costs of production. Arrow also observed that, once information has been produced, there is no cost to give it to any additional user. When a pay television company charges a subscriber seven dollars to view a certain motion picture, many people who might have gladly paid a smaller sum will choose not to see the film. In the crisp calculus of twentieth-century economics, this is undesirable because it decreases the welfare of one class of consumers—the excluded viewers—without increasing the welfare of another—those willing and able to pay the asking price.

The dilemma for public policy is that if society withholds property rights from creative work, the price that its producers can charge for access to it will begin to approach zero; their revenues will diminish and, with them, their incentives to produce more. But if society confers property rights on creative works, prices will rise and the information produced will reach smaller, wealthier (or more profligate) audiences, even though it might be that the work could be disseminated to everyone else at no additional cost.

At bottom, the problem is that, in many instances in intellectual, literary, and educational life, information and entertainment are costly to produce but cheap to distribute. One solution to the problem is to have governments subsidize the creative work it believes the public wants, and then distribute free copies of the works produced. The public would of course pay in the form of higher taxes, but these payments would be unconnected to any particular value a work might have for any particular taxpayer. For example, if the income tax was used to pay for these subsidies, the rich would effectively pay a greater share of the cost than the poor. (The U.S. Copyright Act in fact approximates this subsidy solution by withholding copyright from works of the U.S. government, such as Commerce Department census reports.)

Few disagree with Arrow's analysis of the public policy problem that intellectual property presents. But one economist, Harold Demsetz, bristled at the suggestion that government subsidies could solve the problem. For Demsetz, an economics professor at the University of Chicago, it is not sufficient to lament, as Arrow did, the failings of free markets. Market failures must be weighed against the shortcomings of government subsidy, and for Demsetz, the deficiencies of private property rights are less baleful than the hazards of public intervention. Demsetz started from the by now familiar point that, as he put it, "it is hardly useful to say that there is 'underutilization' of information if the method recommended to avoid 'underutilization' discourages the research required to produce the information." But he gave the argument a distinctive twist. The production and consumption of information, he argued, cannot be judged independently of each other. Producers produce what consumers will pay for, in the case of intellectual goods no less than in the case of breakfast cereals and automobiles. While charging for access to these goods might seem a bad thing to Arrow, prices do have the salutary effort of signaling consumer preference and channeling private investment in the right directions.

Demsetz's disagreement with Arrow was not that he reached the wrong conclusions but that he did not reach far enough; he failed to pin his conclusions to marketplace realities. Whatever the theoretical failings of private property rights in intellectual goods, they do have the virtue of revealing at least some information about consumer preferences, information that government subsidy systems at best imperfectly collect. The logic of property rights dictates their extension into every corner in which people derive enjoyment and value from literary and artistic works. To stop short of these ends would deprive producers of the signals of consumer preference that trigger and direct their investments. Viewed through these lenses, two hundred years of practical intuition and economic analysis in England and the United States have produced exactly the same prescription that natural rights theory has produced on the Continent: copyright should extend into every corner of economic value where the cost of negotiating a license is not insurmountably high.

If the practical workings and underlying rationales of the two cultures of copyright have so much in common, what explains the persistence of their conflicting symbols—robust authorial rights pitted against stinting utilitarianism? One answer is that the symbols fit well in their respective national cultures. It is no less comforting for an American lawmaker to consider his efforts as exemplifying hard-nosed (if unexamined) utilitarianism than for a French legislator to wrap his efforts in the romantic trappings of an author's natural rights. Also, symbols have great—and malleable—political power. In the world of American copyright politics, in which consensus among competing interest groups has become the dominant legislative method, a rationale that purports to balance the strictly assessed economic interests of producers and consumers seems useful.

Nowhere are the national symbols of author's rights and copyright wielded to greater effect than in international copyright relations. It is probably no coincidence that the French became so committed to the idea of author's rights at about the time that international piracy of French books began to flourish, when some principle was required that would establish respect for the economic interests in French works abroad. And it may also be no coincidence that the United States at the same time defended its refusal to honor rights in foreign works on pragmatic, utilitarian grounds: it was then more an importer than an exporter of intellectual goods. But as the balance of copyright trade has shifted, and Europe has become a net importer of American works, copyright symbols are once again being manipulated in order to obtain trade advantages.

International copyright is at once dazzlingly complex and brutally simple. For a lawmaker in Country A, the knee-jerk answer to the question whether Country A should give copyright protection to works coming from Country B is simple: it should not. The effect would be to raise the price that Country A's citizens must pay for literary and artistic works from Country B above what they would be if the works were not protected by copyright; at least part of that price would leave Country A in the form of royalties paid to copyright owners in Country B. From Country A's perspective, wealth staying in the country is considered better than wealth flowing out of it, so the better course would be to deny copyright protection to Country B's works.

Belgium followed this policy in the early nineteenth century by refusing to protect works from its larger and wealthy neighbor France, thus ensuring its citizens a steady and bountiful supply of French books at prices lower than they would have to pay if Belgium had given the books copyright protection. The history of this experience shows, however, that simple prescriptions do not always work. Belgian publishers, able to print and sell works by French authors without any obligation to pay royalties, understandably enough declined to publish French-language manuscripts from *Belgian* writers, who would get a royalty. The Belgian authors pressed their government to level the playing field by extending copyright to works from France. France, meanwhile, concerned about the revenues lost to French authors and publishers, pushed for and eventually got a copyright treaty between the two countries: in the future, each would give copyright protection to the works of the other's authors.

The copyright treaty between France and Belgium rested on the principle of reciprocity. France would, within its borders, protect works coming from Belgium to the same extent that Belgium, within its borders, protected works coming from France; similarly, Belgium would give French works the same protection that France gave to Belgian works. (One international copyright lawyer has defined the principle of reciprocity as "I'll scratch your back if you scratch mine—but not necessarily in the same place.")

Reciprocity rarely offers both sides an equally good deal. If Country A imports more literary and artistic works from Country B than it exports to Country B, it will be better off denying protection to works written by Country B's authors even if that means forgoing protection for its own writers in Country B. Or if, unlike Belgium in the nineteenth century, Country A doesn't have many publishers who would suffer competition from cheap imports, it has even greater reason, at least for the short term, to reject reciprocal copyright treaty relations. (A long-term consequence is that, becoming a haven for unprotected foreign work, it may keep itself from developing a significant publishing industry of its own.)

Several nations initially concluded that reciprocal copyright relations were a bad bargain, and they declined to join France at the treaty table. Then, in 1852, France announced a bold initiative resting squarely on the doctrine of author's rights: France would extend copyright not only to works coming from countries, like Belgium, that agreed to protect French works, but also to works from countries that did not. What more powerful endorsement of the universal rights of authors could a nation offer than this selfless, possibly unrequited, embrace of literary work regardless of nationality? The gesture also had its pragmatic purpose, of course, for it might embarrass other nations into agreeing to protect French works; indeed, within ten years, twenty-three countries had signed copyright treaties with France. And, at the least, the new law stabilized book prices in France, since publishers no longer engaged in cutthroat competition between foreign and domestic titles.

As a nation that was just beginning to develop a literary tradition of its own and that was overwhelmingly a net importer of books (from England), the United States from the start refused to protect foreign works, even if this meant that American works were unprotected abroad and that domestic publishers had to compete among themselves over cheap editions of foreign works. Pressures to extend American copyright to foreign authors first developed in the 1830s, as American writers and some American publishers, together with English ones, pressed for a bilateral treaty between the United States and England. (Charles Dickens traveled to the United States in 1842 to proselytize for international copyright.) But arrayed against them were American printers already protected by a high tariff on imported books, who had no desire to pay royalties to English writers or publishers. "Customary copyrights," called "trade courtesy," under which these pirating publishers deferred to each other's first printing of an English work, helped to stave off ruinous price wars among them over popular books.

At the same time that the United States was refusing protection on any terms for foreign literary works, several countries in Europe were moving away from reciprocity to the more cosmopolitan and efficient treaty principle of "national treatment." Unlike reciprocity, national treatment would obligate each nation that signs the treaty to protect works produced by nationals of all other treaty members on the same terms that it protects the works of its own nationals. Thus, a Belgian suing for copyright infringement in France would get the same protection that France gives its own nationals, not the protection that Belgium gives to French nationals. Taken by itself, this principle may offer little comfort to Country C, which has major copyright industries and a comprehensive copyright statute that protects all forms of literary and artistic works. Country D, with many poets but few composers, could enact a law that protected poetry but excluded protection for musical works, with the result that listeners in Country D would hear music from Country C for free, while Country D's poets and composers would both get full protection in Country C. To forestall such a lopsided allocation of rights, the more pragmatic advocates proposed that the national treatment principle be allied with a system of minimum standards: a member country would be free to treat the copyrighted work of its own nationals in any way it chose, but in dealing with works from other treaty members it would have to abide by certain minimum treaty standards— among them a comprehensive definition of copyright subject matter that included both poetry and musical works.

In 1884, after twenty-five years of meetings among publishers, academics, and writers—Victor Hugo was prominent in them—diplomats from ten countries met in Berne, Switzerland, to begin mapping out the terms of a multilateral copyright treaty that would rest on the principle of national treatment with minimum standards. The treaty, signed in 1886, had France, Germany, and the United Kingdom, but not the United States, among its founding members. American representatives had attended the Berne conferences only as observers, and gave no hint that their government would sign the treaty in the future. The very first United States copyright act, in 1790, had expressly permitted "the importation or vending, reprinting or publishing within the United States, of any map, chart, book or books, written, printed, or published by any person not a citizen of the United States," and the country remained unwilling to move from this position.

Five years passed before the United States took its first, grudging step to protect foreign works. The Chace Act, passed in 1891, empowered the President to extend copyright to works of foreign nationals, but it did so in a mostly illusory way. Ever since 1790, the United States had imposed formalities—notice, registration, and deposit—as a condition to copyright protection, in part on the utilitarian premise that compliance with formalities is a good litmus test of an author's intention to claim protection for his work. The Chace Act now imposed these formalities on foreign publishers as well and added a special requirement for them, the so-called manufacturing clause, which required all copies of foreign literary works to be printed from type set in the United States if they were to have American protection—an obvious concession to American printers, who might otherwise have opposed the Act.

For the next century, the relationship between the United States and the Berne Union was that between reluctant lover and increasingly demanding suitor. Each successive revision of the Berne Convention, in 1908, 1928, 1948, and 1971, imposed higher minimum standards. For example, where the original 1886 Berne text had permitted treaty members to impose formalities as a condition for obtaining copyright protection, the 1908 revision outlawed formalities, and this remained a stumbling block with the United States for more than eighty years. Formalities, and especially the manufacturing clause, persisted in America not on utilitarian grounds but because powerful lobbying groups, such as the printers' and bookbinders' unions, opposed repeated efforts, begun in 1922, to conform the Copyright Act to Berne's requirements.

Toward the end of World War II, when the United States was becoming a major exporter of copyrighted materials, new pressures began to mount for American adherence to a multilateral copyright treaty, and in 1947 the United States indeed proposed one, the Universal Copyright Convention, which would accommodate all cultures of copyright. The idea was to impose only a bland requirement that member countries provide for the "adequate and effective protection" of the rights of authors and other copyright owners; formalities would be tolerated, but the simple act of affixing a copyright notice on copies of a work would substitute for compliance with the remaining American formalities, including the domestic manufacturing requirement. Only the printing unions opposed the new treaty, and ratified in 1954, it came into force in 1955.

Many nations that belonged to the Berne Convention—France, West Germany, and Japan, among them—also signed the Universal Copyright Convention. Under the national treatment principle, this meant that American authors and publishers might get the same level of protection in those countries that the countries gave their own nationals, without any obligation for the United States to reciprocate. Also, a provision of the Berne Convention—the so-called back door to Berne—enabled them to get high-level Berne treatment worldwide by the simple expedient of publishing simultaneously in the United States and in a Berne country such as Canada. (This is one of the reasons so many American books of the era bear the legend "Published simultaneously in Canada.")

Still more pressure for the United States to adhere to the Berne Convention developed when the 1909 Copyright Act was revised in 1976. The revised law phased out the protectionist manufacturing clause, loosened the notice formality, and introduced a copyright term measured by the Berne minimum of the author's life plus fifty years. Then, in the 1980s, Americans began to realize that the United States was a copyright outcast, and that its failure to join the Berne Union was undermining its efforts to negotiate trade agreements that protected American intellectual property in other countries. Secretary of Commerce Malcolm Baldrige testified at congressional hearings that Berne membership would strengthen America's hand, and finally, on March 1, 1989, the United States formally adhered to the Berne Convention for the Protection of Literary and Artistic Works.

Adherence to the Berne Convention raised a new and troubling question for American copyright owners: Is any convention that is willing to have the United States as a member a convention worth joining? From the beginning, the genius of the Berne Convention has been not only to tie together the sometimes disparate laws of member countries but also, however gradually, to raise the standards of protection in all. Sometimes the stretch may seem too great. For example, when Arpad Bogsch, director general of the World Intellectual Property Organization, which administers the

Berne Convention, testified in May 1985 as the lead-off witness at Senate hearings on U.S. adherence to Berne, he suggested that the United States Copyright Act, even with several provisions prohibited by Berne, already met Berne's minimum standards. Bogsch, for years a dominating figure in international copyright, obviously had the longer term in view, for Berne's genius as a rising tide soon became evident in the United States. In adhering to the treaty, and in the years since, Congress has substantially amended the Copyright Act in the direction of complying with Berne's standards.

The great weakness of the Berne Convention—some would call it a strength—and of the Universal Copyright Convention as well is that adherence to its principle of national treatment is essentially an act of faith, faith that other member countries will extend copyright protection to the works of foreigners on at least the minimum terms in the treaty. There are no real enforcement procedures or sanctions; although the Berne Convention allows a member nation to file suit in the International Court of Justice against an offending member, none has ever done so. And in countries that are net importers of copyrighted works, there is a strong temptation to cheat if the benefits of having free access to both domestic and foreign works outweigh the benefits that national authors would gain from the extension of protection to local and foreign authors alike.

The first breach in the international copyright faith began to appear in the late 1950s. Nations newly independent of European colonial powers—India was the most vocal—chafed at being held to the standards of treaties to which their former masters had committed them. They eventually threatened to defect from both Berne and the Universal Copyright Convention. The preamble to recommendations adopted at a

1963 African Study Meeting on Copyright in Brazzaville, Congo, declared that "international copyright conventions are designed, in their present form, to meet the needs of countries which are exporters of intellectual works. These conventions, if they are to be generally and universally applied, require review and re-examination in the light of the specific needs of the African continent." The insurgents shrewdly focused their demands on the most compelling social claim: unfettered use of copyrighted works for educational and scholarly purposes. And the evident strategy was to threaten turmoil in international copyright—the operative, feared word in the West was "destabilization."

In 1967, the Berne countries met in Stockholm to address these new demands. To the surprise of the Western nations, the insurgents succeeded in obtaining agreement on a Protocol Regarding Developing Countries that would keep them in Berne but substantially reduce their obligation to comply with its minimum requirements by shortening the required minimum term of copyright by twenty-five years and allowing them, upon payment of "equitable remuneration," to reproduce foreign works for "educational or cultural purposes" and to broadcast or translate them.

The Stockholm Protocol put the United States in an uncomfortable position. After more than a century as an international copyright pirate, and still a good distance from Berne, it was also a major copyright exporter with a strong economic interest in the educational and scholarly texts to which the African, Asian, and Latin American countries wanted freer access. When, in December 1967, the Register of Copyrights implored a joint Berne–UCC meeting in Geneva to reverse "the dangerous erosion of authors' rights that seems to be taking place internationally," the irony could not have been lost on his audience. The United States, that notorious copyright pirate and advocate of pragmatic utilitarianism, had suddenly appropriated as its own the rallying symbol—authors—of the old-line Berne countries.

The United States took the lead in pressing for a compromise, hosting a joint Berne–UCC meeting in Washington, D.C., in September 1969. The Washington Recommendation that came out of these meetings laid the basis for the ultimate resolution of the conflict in Paris in 1971, a compromise that raised the level of copyright protection which Universal Copyright Convention members must provide (by saying that "adequate and effective protection" included exclusive rights in reproduction, broadcasting, and public performance) and at the same time relaxed the standards of both the UCC and Berne by saying that its members could translate or reproduce copyrighted works for purposes of teaching, scholarship, or research if licenses were obtained and reasonable remuneration paid.

Attacks on a treaty's minimum requirements are rarely as direct as the aborted Stockholm Protocol. The more subtle temptation to cheat emerges when a new kind of product, or a new technological use of a copyrighted work, creates the opportunity to have the best of both worlds: to collect royalties on the domestic use of both foreign and domestic products, but pay royalties only to one's own nationals. Starting in the mid-1960s, new technologies provided just such an opportunity—tape recording of cassettes on home audio equipment—and statutory systems for collecting royalties on homemade tapes provided the means. But this time it was not the United States, or traditional pirate countries or the developing countries of the Third World, that seized the opportunity. The new chiselers were the old European stalwarts of the

Berne Union, who shrewdly manipulated the slogan of author's rights to achieve protectionist ends.

In the spring of 1993, Mihály Ficsor, director of the World Intellectual Property Organization's Copyright Department, went to Washington to testify before the House Intellectual Property Subcommittee about the vexed issue of national treatment. "Since 1971," he began, "no revision of the Berne Convention has taken place, although during the more than two decades since then, perhaps more important developments have taken place in the creation, dissemination and conditions of protection of works than between the adoption of the Convention and its last revision in 1971." He had in mind the digital and other technologies that were rapidly bringing copyrighted works into homes across the world. And by "conditions of protection" Ficsor evidently meant that substantial revenues from new home-taping charges were already being diverted away from the authors and owners of the copyrighted works and into the pockets of individuals and companies in the countries where the works were being copied.

Another witness at the hearings, Robert Hadl, vice president and general counsel of the entertainment conglomerate MCA, put it differently. "Economic protectionism is rearing its ugly head," he said, "in some countries where imports of copyrighted works are far exceeding exports. This new wave of protectionism has resulted in an abandonment of national treatment in those countries where payments to U.S. nationals, under newly created rights, would exceed payments to their own nationals. States have adopted reciprocity, new concepts of formalities such as 'first fixation,' distinctions based on neighboring rights versus copyright, cultural fund deductions, and 'quotas,' all designed to restrict payments to U.S. nationals."

The Two Cultures of Copyright

Part of the problem was that while Berne and the Universal Copyright Convention require national treatment for author's rights or copyright, lawyers can—and do—disagree on whether a given right in fact is an author's right or copyright. Several nations have public lending rights that compensate authors when their books are borrowed from public libraries. Is this public lending right part of the author's rights guaranteed by Berne? (Only Germany has concluded that it is.) If so, all nationals of Berne member states, wherever they reside, are entitled to share in public lending revenues. Or are the public lending fees merely a form of government subsidy to local authors? (The United Kingdom, among other nations, thinks so.) If so, no obligation exists to share the proceeds with foreigners.

Rights that fall outside the definition of author's right or copyright are not the only sources of value that escape the national treatment requirement. The Berne Convention requires its members to protect only "works" and "authors." If, for some reason, a given product does not qualify as a "work" or if its creator does not qualify as an "author," it, too, may escape national treatment. Is a singer or musician an "author"? Is a recording of a performance a "work"? The United States Copyright Act says they are; continental author's right doctrine says they are not. The result of these discrepant characterizations is a lopsided allocation of international copyright revenues, with Country A getting protection for its nationals' goods in Country B, while Country B's nationals get no protection for the very same goods in Country A.

The difference in national approaches to products such as sound recordings stems from an important, residual difference between the two cultures of copyright. The essentially utilitarian American culture asks not whether there is an author or work, but only whether copyright is needed to ensure the production and dissemination of information and entertainment products. United States copyright law thus tends to bring all literary and artistic creations, including sound recordings, within the scope of copyright; the principle of national treatment consequently makes the United States protect foreign sound recordings under copyright even though the nation where the recording was made—France, for example—may not extend copyright to sound recordings and thus is not obligated to protect them when they come from the United States.

The rejection of protection for products like sound recordings in nations that adhere to the doctrine of author's rights did not begin as a brazen strategy to avoid payments to foreign nationals. Rather, it emerged out of two principles of the author's rights doctrine: only flesh-and-blood authors, not corporate entities such as motion picture studios or record companies, qualify for copyright protection; and if a work is to get this protection, it must be truly creative, revealing the "impress of the author's personality." Although sound recordings or television or radio broadcasts might lack the creative personal element required for the invocation of author's rights, these nations still had an interest in nurturing their domestic recording and broadcast industries and wanted to give them some form of intellectual property protection. The answer was a new system of intellectual property, "neighboring rights"—so called because these diluted, low-rise rights merely border on the cathedral of author's rights.

The evolution of the idea of neighboring rights—from being a doctrine intended to fill a gap left by the rigorous author's rights theory to being a protectionist canard—was gradual. It began with photography, the first technology to challenge the author's rights culture. Europeans ultimately finessed the question of whether these technically created images were "works" by simply calling the photographer an author and finding the impress of his personality in the photographic image. Motion pictures proved only slightly harder to bring within author's rights. Sound recordings finally pressed European lawmakers to the verge. Performers and studio musicians might in a pinch be called authors. But what of record producers and recording technicians? Live radio and television broadcasts, although they called for creativity in editing and production, also appeared to dwell outside the cathedral of author's rights. The solution was to declare that rights in sound recordings and broadcasts were not author's rights at all, but neighboring rights.

Once a nation characterizes a right in some product as a neighboring right, it is free to treat it as it wishes, with no obligations under either the Berne Convention or the Universal Copyright Convention. If, for example, a country requires a royalty to be paid on audio copying equipment and blank tapes, it can distribute the sound recording royalty revenues exclusively to its own nationals, even if most of the copies were of foreign recordings. It can also dip into the pot for its own ends—to subsidize its own authors and artists, for example. It will be constrained only by its sense of good domestic policy, by treaty restrictions other than those of Berne or the UCC, and by considerations of international comity. The Rome Convention for the Protection of Performers, Producers of Phonograms and Broadcasting Organizations (which the United States has not joined) is one source of international obligations.

France's 1985 home-taping law, which imposes a statutory royalty on the sale of blank audiotapes and videotapes, is a good example of how a nation can use the idea of neighboring rights to promote its domestic economy at the expense of foreign creators. The French law first deducts twenty-five percent of the royalties from the home-taping pool for French social and cultural purposes. (These might include subsidies to French filmmakers.) It then divides what is left in three—one-third each to the composer of the musical composition, the performers, and the producer. Because musical compositions are Berne "works," American composers, as their "authors," are entitled under the Berne Convention to share in the third allocated to composers. But since neither performers nor producers are "authors" and since the United States is not a party to the Rome Convention, Americans have no claim to the performers' or producers' thirds, which in France are the subject only of neighboring rights.

France's private copy law offers one narrow alternative to American performers and producers: they can share in the tape revenues if their sound recording or film was first "fixed"—i.e., recorded—in France. The French domestic fixation requirement for films and records is the Gallic twin of the old American manufacturing clause in the copyright law. It is a blatantly protectionist measure aimed at supporting the local record and motion picture industry; like the American manufacturing requirement, it is so onerous that it is unlikely to attract many takers. A fixation requirement is, of course, a formality that Berne would not tolerate—except that, since it applies to a neighboring right, not an author's right, Berne prohibitions do not apply.

From the American perspective—copyright pirate turned prince—the drama of international copyright protection is poignant, indeed. After a century with no foreign copyright relations, the United States grudgingly opened its doors to bilateral arrangements, but on onerous terms. Sixty years later, an accelerating, positive balance of copyright trade pushed it in the direction of Berne, while its formality-ridden copyright statute held it back. No sooner did the United States succeed in promoting the low-level Universal Copyright Convention than the Third World countries threatened to defect. And when, in 1989, the United States finally entered the Berne Union, it was only to discover some of Berne's oldest members assiduously sweeping the choicest morsels off the table.

The American response to what MCA's Robert Hadl called "this new wave of protectionism" has been twofold. One step has been to support efforts begun by the World Intellectual Property Organization to strengthen the national treatment standard. The other, pursued by the Office of the United States Trade Representative, has been to press the general trade negotiation process, such as the General Agreement on Tariffs and Trade, to adopt more evenhanded national treatment standards.

Viewed in the long perspective, the current protectionist surge in international copyright relations is nothing new. From the very first French–Belgian treaty and the early American refusal to undertake international copyright obligations, copyright has been a protectionist card that nations play according to their current notion of what arrangements will best promote the national interest.

Today's worshippers in the Berne cathedral have very different visions of paradise. For Americans, it is a place where the economic logic of rights extending against every new and valuable technological use of copyrighted works is respected by every other Berne adherent. For the Europeans, and other net importers of copyrighted works, it is a smaller place, where the subject matter and rights covered by copyright are confined to their traditional patterns, with no room for newer technologies, such as home taping, that are better left to neighboring rights. The most striking feature of these competing visions is the extent to which they have been assimilated into the accepted symbols of copyright's two cultures, the flinty utilitarianism of the Americans and the author-centered natural rights theorizing of the Europeans.

Over the past century, copyright has gradually extended its reach, both domestically and worldwide. Domestically, new uses—whether translation, dramatization, photocopying, or home taping—have triggered these extensions. Internationally, treaty relations have captured copyright's value in foreign markets. Nations have deftly juggled their symbols of copyright and author's right to rationalize both the domestic expansion of rights and shifting postures in international trade. The recent introduction of copyright into the general trade process, in which new rights can be facilely traded for subsidies to rice and rapeseed oil, promises to complicate both domestic and international copyright, and possibly to diminish the power of their competing symbols. The technology that will galvanize these changes is the celestial jukebox.

CHAPTER SIX

The Celestial Jukebox

One of the transforming scientific revolutions of the twentieth century has been to capture words, sounds, and images in digital form. Technologies exist today that can reduce a written or spoken line of poetry, the subtlest shadings of a musical phrase, a fleeting image captured on film, to the crisp zeros and ones of digital code. By most accounts—some doubtless overblown—most of tomorrow's entertainment and information products will be recorded digitally, stored digitally, transmitted digitally, and received digitally. The digital revolution promises both new strains and new opportunities for copyright law, domestically and worldwide.

Three attributes make the digital form all but irresistible: fidelity, compression, and malleability. A musical performance recorded on a digital compact disc possesses a measure of clarity and durability that far exceeds analog recordings on audiocassettes or vinyl records. A single compact disc, thinner and no wider than a saucer, can digitally compress every word and picture now printed in a twenty-six-volume encyclopedia, with a dictionary and world atlas thrown in as a bonus.

197

The digital format also makes it easier to alter and integrate different art forms. Not only can a silent black-and-white movie be colorized and enhanced with sound sampled from a digital catalogue, but the images of the actors can also be altered—to make them older or younger—and actors from different films from a different generation can, once reduced to a digital common denominator of zeros and ones, be seamlessly integrated into the new work.

One attraction of the digital form transcends all others: its accessibility to the power of the modern digital computer. Computers, whether huge scientific or business mainframes or small personal laptops, already dominate much of business life. Computers in the future will also increasingly negotiate personal encounters with the new digital environment. Because computers operate and communicate only in the zeros and ones of digital code, any product that pins its success on access to computers will need to be cast in digital form.

The prospects for an encompassing digital environment are closer than anyone would have thought a few years ago. Regulatory and technical hurdles are rapidly disappearing. In the United States, the breakup of AT&T's telephone monopoly in 1984 produced intense competition—and occasional alliances—between cable systems and regional telephone companies to control the new communications infrastructure. Digital signal compression makes it possible for the telephone companies' antiquated, twisted pairs of copper wire to carry the expected traffic of two-way, interactive uses, ranging from the instantaneous selection of films or sound recordings, to the examination and purchase of merchandise from a home-shopping network, to a telescoping access to the on-the-scene news reporting that lies behind edited news reports. Fiber optic networks, which can enable these interactive uses even without compression, already link business users in many big cities; once extended into the home, they will have the capacity to transmit five hundred television channels or more. Internet, an international computer network, today links the digital messages of millions of users.

The metaphor that best expresses the possibilities of the future is the celestial jukebox, a technology-packed satellite orbiting thousands of miles above Earth, awaiting a subscriber's order—like a nickel in the old jukebox, and the punch of a button—to connect him to any number of selections from a vast storehouse via a home or office receiver that combines the power of a television set, radio, CD player, VCR, telephone, fax, and personal computer. Today the celestial jukebox is only a metaphor; its infrastructure—much of which will certainly be earthbound—is far from complete. But the pace of technological development is so fast and the forces of market demand so strong that the celestial jukebox, however configured, will be in place sometime early in the twenty-first century.

Interactivity between users and creators is an important feature of the celestial jukebox. Pay television, which has for years enabled subscribers to order up movies or programs for delivery at scheduled times, is a signpost pointing to a future in which information and entertainment products will be available on demand; so are the elaborate switching mechanisms that make telephone conversations possible. The child's play of video games points to a time when subscribers will be able to manipulate the digital bits and pieces stored in the celestial jukebox to create their own individualized works.

From today's vantage point, the celestial jukebox may seem to offer only a convenient new way to disseminate works that were initially conceived as—and are already available in retail outlets for—books, records, or videocassettes. But soon it may be more like a warehouse filled with fragments of recorded sound, visual images, and printed material that electronically cruising subscribers can combine and recombine to their own tastes and purposes. If that happens, the celestial jukebox will bring copyright closer than ever to its historic economic objects. Since the Statute of Anne, copyright has aimed at subjecting the production of literary and artistic works to the discipline of market forces; because the celestial jukebox can keep a record of every selection a subscriber makes, and the price he paid for it, copyright owners will have a far more precise measure of the demand for their products than they do today. This capacity should enable them to channel their investments more precisely to meet these newly articulated patterns of demand.

Will copyright be able to serve every corner of the celestial jukebox? Historically, it has protected finished works—the "Writings" of "Authors" contemplated by the United States Constitution. In some cases, the most popular uses of these works will remain entirely outside the celestial jukebox. Books—particularly fiction—will continue to flourish as they have since before the Statute of Anne. Readers are not likely to give up the determinate pleasures of a volume they can carry with them, knowing that when the book ends the story ends. Copyright faces no new challenge in serving the palpable pleasures of the book and other such finite products either inside or out of the celestial jukebox.

But much of the value of the celestial jukebox will lie in indeterminate objects, in processes and data rather than in finished works, in the computer programs and fragments of information and entertainment that subscribers will manipulate to make something original of their own. Patent law and unfair competition law are better designed than copyright law to protect processes and data, but they have fallen short in giving these dynamic elements the protection they need. American courts have episodically expanded copyright beyond its traditional boundaries to fill these intellectual property gaps. Which result is better: adequate protection for computer programs and data, but a distended copyright; or a traditionally configured copyright, but underinvestment in computer programs and data?

The new digital environment will place another strain on copyright. Most uses of the celestial jukebox will take place in the privacy of the home, a trend that began in the mid-1960s when home audiotaping and then videotaping started to displace revenues earned in the retail marketplace of movie theaters, videocassette stores, and record outlets. But copyright has been primarily a doctrine of public places. The challenge for Congress in the age of the celestial jukebox will be to extend liability against private uses more promptly than it has in the past.

The U.S. Congress is not the only legislature that will face this challenge. The reach of the celestial jukebox will be global. Legal disputes such as Ted Turner's litigation in France over the colorized version of *The Asphalt Jungle* will likely become an ever more regular feature of international copyright business. Nations will also dispute as they try to meet local demand for access to foreign entertainment and at the same time try to reduce imbalances in their copyright trade. One probable result is that the self-contained system of international copyright embodied in the Berne and Universal Copyright Conventions will begin to cede some of its authority to trade arrangements such as GATT.

Two prescriptions for copyright lawmaking stand out. First,

as new forms of technological *subject matter* claim copyright protection, lawmakers should carefully measure them against copyright's historic standards and resist the temptation to extend protection simply because copyright represents the most capacious and catholic intellectual property doctrine. For example, when layouts for semiconductor chips—the bits of silicon smaller than a fingernail that drive everything from computers to automobile carburetors—were first presented to the Copyright Office for registration, that Office had to think hard before accepting them even on the most limited terms. Second, as new technological *uses* of copyrighted works emerge, lawmakers should be quick to extend copyright to encompass them, even if the uses are construed as private. One example is home viewing of films from the celestial jukebox, which under present copyright law a court might be persuaded to consider a "private" rather than a "public" performance and thus exempt from claims for infringement. The lesson of the U.S. Congress's ambivalence over "private" uses that stalled much American copyright lawmaking in the past quarter century is that rights delayed are usually rights denied.

Neither of these prescriptions is radical. Domestically, they simply reflect the abiding logic of American copyright as explicated by the law and economics literature of the 1970s, and the genius of the author's rights doctrine before neighboring rights began in the 1980s to erode its foundations. Internationally, they echo the standards and aspirations of the Berne Convention. Nor are these prescriptions academic. Bruce Springsteen complained in a 1992 song: "57 Channels—And Nothing On." Decisions about the scope of copyright's subject matter and the reach of its rights will inevitably affect the quantity, quality, and cost of future literary and artistic works—and whether, in the future, there is anything on that is worth watching.

When, in May 1964, the United States Copyright Office issued its first registration for a computer program, it was with a mild foreboding that copyright might not be the right form of protection for this new subject matter. Fifty-six years of protection, the then prevailing copyright term, might have seemed too long for such a fast-moving technology. Also, copyright's easygoing standard for protection, evident since Justice Holmes's circus poster decision, might sustain technological monopolies that patent law, with its more rigorous standards, would consign to the public domain. But an overarching confidence prevailed that traditional doctrine would smooth over any rough edges. In the panglossian spirit of the day, Deputy Register of Copyrights George Cary observed, "Basically, a computer program is a set of instructions; it might be likened to a 'How to Do It' book."

But copyright as correctly applied will not protect the most valuable element of these products—*how* to do it. American courts have withheld copyright protection from utilitarian processes and methods at least since 1879, when the Supreme Court ruled that although the author of a text explaining a new system of bookkeeping could get copyright for the precise words he used to explain his system, only patent law could protect the system itself. Congress expressly codified this rule when it passed the 1976 Copyright Act, which specifies that copyright does not extend to any "idea, procedure, process, system, method of operation, concept, principle, or discovery."

Patent law, with its rigorous rights but equally rigorous standards and its comparatively short—seventeen-year—term, is better calibrated to encourage investments in technological inventions, while at the same time keeping unwarranted monopolies out of the marketplace. However, the Patent Office was unprepared for the onslaught of new software patent applications that swamped it in the 1980s, and the patent system itself was hostile to the needs of software producers: patent examiners expert in software were hard to find; information on the "prior art," against which to measure a computer program's inventiveness, was sparse; the patent examination process could consume tens of thousands of dollars and three years or more—in many cases, much more—often longer than the useful life of the program; and few of the patents the Office issued could expect to hold up against challenge in court. Not surprisingly, software producers willing to commit the fate of their programs to the patent system were relatively scarce.

Copyright for computer programs was far more attractive: for the twenty dollars it costs to obtain a copyright registration certificate, one could get immediate access to federal courts and the extensive array of legal remedies against copyright infringement—injunctions, impoundment and destruction of infringing copies, statutory damages, and attorney's fees—without having to go through a lengthy or searching patent examination process. Still, no software producer could realistically expect copyright to protect the most innovative, functional elements of his products, the methods and processes that enable users to harness the computer's power. Nonetheless, throughout the 1980s, many software producers cast their fortunes with copyright, hoping that the law's easygoing, Holmesian embrace, when coupled with a judicial instinct to extend copyright where no other form of protection was at hand, would protect the investments made in their programs' underlying methods.

For a time, some courts requited these hopes. In 1986, in the first major judicial ruling on the scope of copyright protection for computer programs, a federal appeals court ruled that the copyright in a computer program for managing dental laboratories covered not only the exact lines of the program's code but also the program's "structure, sequence and organization." The program's *only* unprotectible element, the court said, was its seminal concept—"the efficient organization of a dental laboratory." Though perhaps achieving a kind of rough justice, the decision departed sharply from a century of copyright jurisprudence. If a court were to treat a traditional literary work like *Romeo and Juliet* in the same way, it would have to hold, against all precedent, that copyright protected every element in the play—character types, historical incidents, very old plot devices—other than the play's most basic concept of star-crossed lovers who belonged to rival families.

Copyright law has a youthful capacity to self-correct. Within a few years, almost every federal appeals courts that addressed the question of copyright protection for computer programs returned to the mainstream from which the dental laboratory decision had taken a detour. In one widely followed decision, the Second Circuit Court of Appeals ruled that copyright barred competitors from copying the textual content of a computer program's lines of code, but allowed them to copy the underlying elements that were essential to the program's most efficient operation; "the more efficient a set of modules are, the more closely they approximate the idea or process embodied in that particular aspect of the program's structure."

Anyone who has ever used a personal computer or watched a child use one will understandably question whether copyright has in fact failed to protect innovative software. Over the 1980s, when an unprecedented outpouring of highly creative software flooded the market—spreadsheet programs, database managers, desktop publishing programs, and video games—copyright was the most visible source of intellectual property protection for these goods. How deficient can copyright be if it could support investment in such a dazzling array of innovation?

One answer is that it was not copyright that was protecting much of this investment. State trade secret laws were equally if not more important. "Source code"—the form in which programmers write computer programs—is comprehensible to humans but not to the computer that must execute a program. "Object code"—the form to which source code must be converted for it to be executed by a computer—is comprehensible to computers but not to humans. The trick is that software producers commonly market their programs only in the form of indecipherable object code; by guarding the underlying, and comprehensible, source code as a trade secret, they can try to conceal from the prying eyes of competitors the innovative processes and methods at the heart of their programs. Indeed, it is common in the software industry to refer to source code as a company's "crown jewels."

Another answer is that software producers simply misjudged the extent to which copyright protected their innovations, thinking that their strong protectionist *hopes* accurately forecast what the courts would decide. Until judicial decisions in the early 1990s restored copyright protection for computer programs to the law's traditional four corners, it was such persistent hopes that helped to fuel investment in software innovations. Two examples stand out.

In 1984, Apple Computer introduced its phenomenally

successful Macintosh personal computer. One source of its success was the machine's "user friendliness," substituting a visual, intuitively compelling "graphical user interface" for the prescribed lettered or numbered commands a user needs to type in in order to operate the computer. Manipulating a hand-held "mouse," a Macintosh user could direct a cursor on the computer screen to one of several icons. He could, for example, delete a file of information by simply dragging the file-folder icon on the screen to a trash can icon, then clicking the mouse. When Microsoft and Hewlett-Packard introduced similar graphical user interfaces, Windows and New Wave, for use in competing computers, Apple filed suit for infringement of copyright in the "look and feel" of the Macintosh interface.

Apple had marketed the Macintosh under an ingenious strategy. By requiring other software producers who wrote application programs for the Macintosh to use the machine's graphical user interface, Apple enhanced the utility—and consequently sales—of the Macintosh; as sales increased, so did sales of application programs and the incentive to write still more. In short order, the Macintosh interface would become not just an attractive feature but a user habit, much like the nearly universal arrangement of letters on a standard typewriter keyboard that typists had become habituated to. Any competitor with a different graphical interface would have to persuade consumers to break the Macintosh habit and learn to operate a new format. If he tried to overcome this marketing obstacle by simulating the Macintosh interface, he would face a lawsuit for copyright infringement.

In August 1992, San Francisco federal trial judge Vaughn Walker dismantled Apple's copyright strategy. Observing in *Apple v. Microsoft* that "purely functional items or an arrangement of them for functional purposes are wholly beyond the realm of copyright as are other common examples of user interfaces"—such as "the dials, knobs and remote control devices of a television or VCR"—Judge Walker added that "the similarity of such functional elements of a user interface or their arrangement in products of like kind does not suggest unlawful copying but standardization across competing products for functional considerations." To accept Apple's "look and feel" argument, Walker concluded, "would allow it to sweep within its proprietary embrace" not only Windows and New Wave but "also other desktop graphical user interfaces which employ the standardized features of such interfaces and to do this without subjecting Apple's claim of copyright to the scrutiny which courts have historically employed."

If decisions like *Apple v. Microsoft*, rejecting the broad scope of software protection applied in the 1986 dental laboratory case, meant that copyright would not be available to protect a software program's underlying methods and processes, could copyright at least buttress the trade secret strategy? The question gave rise to a hotly contested debate over the permissibility of reverse engineering of computer programs, done to discern a program's underlying, and unprotected, methods and process.

Trade secret law allows competitors to discover a trade secret lawfully, through a process known as reverse engineering—examining a marketed product and subjecting it to chemical or electronic analysis if necessary in order to discern its underlying secrets. (Under trade secret law, anyone is free to analyze a glass of Coca-Cola chemically to figure out its secret formula and then market a soft drink produced according to the deduced formula.) A reverse engineering technique, called disassembly, exists for computer programs by which one can convert a program's object code into comprehensible source code and, once they are apparent, pick out the program's underlying and uncopyrightable methods. But copyright presents a hitch. Disassembly necessarily entails as an initial step that the competitor make at least one copy of the program's entire object code; making that copy could be construed as copyright infringement.

Will copyright law bar disassembly for the limited purpose of discerning a computer program's unprotectible methods and processes? In the 1980s, two large producers of video games and video game consoles, Nintendo of America and Sega Enterprises, tried to put copyright to precisely this end in order to stop competitors from producing video games capable of running on Nintendo and Sega consoles. Their aim was to limit the market for compatible video games to their own products and to products of third-party licensees, who were willing to pay for access to the world's two most popular video game platforms. The strategy of the two companies was to claim copyright in the lines of object code that competitors would have to copy if they wanted their video games to operate on Nintendo and Sega consoles. Effectively the companies were building an electronic lock into their consoles and claiming copyright in the key.

Sega v. Accolade, filed in San Francisco federal district court in October 1991, captured the same intense attention as *Apple v. Microsoft*. In April 1992, the trial judge ruled for Sega and enjoined Accolade, a video game producer, from selling games it had created by first copying and then disassembling the object code of Sega's video game to identify the key that unlocked Sega's Genesis console so that one could play Accolade games on it. The Ninth Circuit Court of Appeals, evidently recognizing the effect the trial court's injunction could have on Accolade's sale of video games during the Christmas season, put the case on a fast track, scheduling argument for July 20. It delivered a unanimous decision three months later, and in terms that covered not just video games but all computer programs. "Where disassembly is the only way to gain access to the ideas and functional elements embodied in a copyrighted computer program and where there is a legitimate reason for seeking such access, disassembly is a fair use of the copyrighted work as a matter of law." Fair use, that safety valve first built into copyright law in the 1841 case about George Washington's letters, and later used to rescue the United States government in *Williams & Wilkins* and Sony in the *Betamax* case, now opened a competitive door for video game and computer companies that wanted to sell digital products that could interoperate with their competitors' products.

Writing for the court, Judge Stephen Reinhardt methodically checked off the Copyright Act's four fair use factors in the well-known section 107. The first factor, the purpose of the defendant's use, weighed in Accolade's favor, since "the use at issue was an intermediate one only and thus any commercial 'exploitation' was indirect or derivative." Although "Accolade's ultimate purpose was the release of Genesis-compatible games for sale, its direct purpose in copying Sega's code, and thus its direct use of the copyrighted material, was simply to study the functional requirements for Genesis compatibility so that it could modify existing games and make them usable with the Genesis console." Further, "no other method of studying those requirements was available to Accolade."

Section 107's second factor, the nature of the copyrighted work, also counted in Accolade's favor. "Because Sega's video game programs contain unprotected aspects that cannot be examined without copying, we afford them a lower degree of protection than more traditional literary works." The third factor—the amount copied from the copyrighted work— weighed against Accolade, because it had copied the entire Sega video game as its first step in disassembly. But the court, citing *Sony*, noted that this alone does not preclude fair use. Finally, on the fourth factor—market effect—the court concluded that there was no basis to assume that defendant's video game significantly affected the market for plaintiff's, "since a consumer might easily purchase both."

By now, copyright's exhausted possibilities for protecting the methods and processes underlying computer programs sparked a renewed interest in patent protection. The early returns were hardly encouraging. When in August 1993 the Patent Office issued Patent Number 5,241,671 to Compton's New Media for a "Multimedia Search System Using a Plurality of Entry Path Means Which Indicate Interrelatedness of Information," an alarmed multimedia community complained not only that the patent was overly broad, sweeping whole fields of current multimedia products within its net, but also that the technology was already well known and for that reason should not enjoy a patent. (Patents are available only for "novel" and "nonobvious" inventions.) In an unusual, and unusually prompt, response to these complaints, the Patent Office announced it would reexamine the patent's validity.

Data and databases, like computer programs, are an important part of the celestial jukebox. And, like computer programs, these products get less protection from copyright than their producers need to support the expense of data collection and assembly. The only copyrightable aspect of a database is the manner in which the data have been selected and

211

arranged; copyright will not protect the data themselves. A restaurant reviewer who goes from one door to the next collecting restaurant names to publish in a dining guide can get no copyright for his efforts. To receive copyright protection, he would have to show some original principle of selection or arrangement of his choices—perhaps according to his personal assessments of quality. Even then, he gets protection *only* for his selection or arrangement. For a database producer, the problem is that, by protecting only the selection and arrangement but not the data themselves, copyright has protection begin at the very point where his investment—the cost of collecting the data in the first place—ends.

Just as a few courts in the early software cases extended copyright to traditionally unprotectible methods and processes, some courts have departed from strict copyright principle to protect database producers for the "sweat of the brow" they invested in collecting data. In one such departure, in 1987, a federal district court in Kansas held that a telephone company that had spent time and money collecting names and telephone numbers for its white page directory was entitled to copyright relief against a competing directory publisher that had copied many of these names and numbers (including a few fictitious listings that the plaintiff had included as a trap to ensnare copiers—a common trick among directory publishers, doubtless to the annoyance of the hungry tourist who discovers that the charming French restaurant listed in his travel guide does not in fact exist).

If *Feist Publications v. Rural Telephone Service* looked as if it involved only the small change of a telephone directory's white pages, the lineup of *amici curiae* who joined the case when it went on appeal to the Supreme Court left no doubt about its importance to the database industry. Among the *am-*

ici were the Information Industry Association, a trade group that represented leading electronic database companies; ADAPSO, an association of more than six hundred companies involved in computers, communications, and data management; the Association of American Publishers; and individual database suppliers such as Mead Data Central and West Publishing.

When the Supreme Court reviewed the Kansas decision in 1991, it dropped a bombshell. Overturning the lower court decision, the Court ruled that not only the Copyright Act but the Constitution itself prohibited the use of copyright to protect the sweat of the brow invested in collecting data. The Court squarely rested its decision for Feist, the copycat publisher, on the proposition that no amount of effort in researching, collecting, or producing data will entitle the results of the effort to copyright protection. While "it may seem unfair that much of the fruit of the compiler's labor may be used by others without compensation," Sandra Day O'Connor wrote, the result "is neither unfair nor unfortunate. It is the means by which copyright advances the progress of science and art." "Creativity" is the key to copyright, whether in selection or arrangement. Acknowledging that alphabetization does constitute an "arrangement," O'Connor concluded that "there is nothing remotely creative about arranging names alphabetically in a white pages directory."

A Supreme Court Justice writing an opinion that interprets a statute narrowly, or that curbs Congress's freedom under a claimed constitutional power, will sometimes subtly counsel Congress on how to repair the omission. Justice Holmes had done this in his opinion in the 1908 pianola case, *White-Smith Music v. Apollo.* Justice O'Connor may have been doing the same in *Feist* when she intimated that, if the Constitution's copyright clause did not authorize protection for data gathering, some other clause, such as the commerce power, might give Congress the needed power. But if Congress heard the message, it did not show the will to act on it.

A goad to congressional action may yet present itself, and from an unexpected quarter—the European Union (formerly called the European Community). On January 29, 1992, the European Commission issued the first draft of a Database Directive to be implemented by member countries no later than January 1, 1995. The proposed directive took a two-tier approach to databases. Copyright is the first tier. If a database producer's selection and arrangement of data show creative authorship, the database will qualify for copyright protection, as it does in the United States. The second tier covers the database's underlying, uncopyrightable data, and gives database suppliers a right, lasting fifteen years, against a competitor's "unfair extraction" of data by rearrangement in different forms. If the database owner has a monopoly over the tools used in collecting its data—a telephone company will often enjoy such a monopoly—the proposed directive would entitle competitors to take the data directly from the database so long as they pay the database owner a reasonable fee.

Because the proposed Database Directive's second tier covers only an uncopyrightable product, its protection lies outside copyright; because it lies outside copyright, it also falls outside the Berne Convention's requirement of national treatment—which would allow the European Union to condition second-tier protection for foreign databases on material reciprocity. ("I'll scratch your back if you scratch mine—but not necessarily in the same place.") The proposed directive's requirement of material reciprocity means that American database producers would be protected in Europe under the directive's second tier only if U.S. law gives comparable protection to European companies in America. The prospect of a lost trade advantage in Europe may well push Congress to pass such a law. And although material reciprocity requires Congress to protect only European, not American, database producers, it is unlikely that Congress would enact a law that protects European companies but not American ones.

No one will seriously argue that investment in computer programs and databases does not require some form of intellectual property protection. The only question is what form of protection will best serve the general welfare. One alternative to the rather thin protection that existing intellectual property laws give to computer programs and databases is a custom-crafted—*sui generis*—intellectual property law designed to meet the special needs of these products. There is ample precedent for such specially crafted laws. The United States Patent Act has *sui generis* provisions for protecting industrial designs, such as chairs and lamp bases, and new varieties of fruits and vegetables. The Semiconductor Chip Protection Act, passed in 1984, is specially tailored to the semiconductor industry's need for protecting the intricate stencils used in manufacturing semiconductor chips. As early as 1969, an IBM lawyer published a proposal for *sui generis* protection for computer programs; the proposal would have extended a different measure of protection to each of a program's three elements—its concepts, documentation, and coded sequences—for a period of five to ten years. The second tier of the proposed EU Database Directive is yet another example of *sui generis* legislation.

Sui generis laws have their detractors, who argue that their narrow focus is a vice, not a virtue. For example, a key provision of the Semiconductor Chip Protection Act was tied to a technology that quickly became obsolete. But this is no argument against the *sui generis* concept itself, since these laws can be amended to accommodate new technologies, just as the subject matter coverage of the Copyright Act has regularly been amended by Congress. Another objection to these laws is that their novelty may disrupt investment in new technologies at the very time investors need certainty the most. But the turbulent history of copyright protection for databases and computer software suggests that a *sui generis* law that aims at a desired level of innovation, and takes into account the special characteristics of its subject matter, will, however uncertain its outcome, outperform a copyright law whose undifferentiated embrace and low level of protection are of little benefit.

If Congress should move selectively in bringing new subject matter into copyright, it should move promptly and comprehensively to bring new technological uses of literary and artistic works under copyright control. The reason lies in the politics of entrenchment. The history of legislative efforts to bring private uses such as home audiotaping and videotaping within copyright control teaches that once a new technology is widespread, and individuals get accustomed to using it for free, it is virtually impossible to get Congress to prohibit its use. And when Congress equivocates on liability, Supreme Court decisions of the last quarter century indicate that the Court will refuse to interpret ambiguous statutory language as encompassing new technological uses. (This judicial restraint appears to be entirely independent of the Court's political composition.) But markets for new uses can substantially, if not completely, displace markets for old uses. Uncontrolled use in new markets not only can deprive producers of the revenues they need to continue doing their work but may also muffle the signals they need to hear about popular preference. No one, not even the most ardent copyright pessimist, has sought to rebut the argument that the production and consumption of information are connected, and that there is no better way for the public to indicate what they want than through the price they are willing to pay in the marketplace. Uncompensated use inevitably dilutes these signals.

Historically, Congress has declined to extend copyright to protect against private uses because transaction costs—the costs to copyright owners and users of locating and negotiating with each other—as a practical matter prevent them from entering into a copyright license. (William Passano spent fifty dollars to collect ten, but only to establish a legal principle, not as a general business practice.) Section 108's exemption for library photocopying, and the fair use doctrine as applied in the *Williams & Wilkins* and Betamax cases, each show copyright law's response to the problem of transaction costs. Recognizing that these costs hobble negotiated licenses, Congress and the courts excuse the otherwise infringing use of copyrighted material, on the pragmatic ground that society is better off getting half a loaf (free use, but no payment to the copyright owner) than getting no loaf at all (no use and no payment).

The Copyright Act's limitation of liability to "public" performances is another example of sensitivity about transaction costs. The reason Congress decided not to impose copyright liability on children singing "Happy Birthday" at a party had less to do with its concern for privacy than with its recognition that identifying and negotiating over such dispersed, ephemeral uses was expensive and unlikely. Television and radio broadcasts come within the Copyright Act's definition of public performance because it is easy to impose liability on a relatively small, and easily identified, number of broadcasters. But will courts call it a public performance when a copyrighted work is not broadcast simultaneously to a large public but rather is transmitted, one performance at a time, to subscribers on demand?

Transaction costs as a prescription for copyright policy can become an obsession. Congress and courts often act as if transaction costs are immutable when, in fact, they are highly contingent. Indeed, the very decision to extend copyright into corners where transaction costs appear to be insuperably high may galvanize the market forces needed to reduce transaction costs. Had Justice Holmes not persuaded his fellow Justices that all commercial performances are "for profit" under the 1909 Copyright Act, Victor Herbert would have lost his lawsuit against Shanley's Restaurant and ASCAP would have encountered a difficult obstacle in its efforts to license the new technology of radio broadcasts. The Society, already struggling, might well have dissolved, and the transaction costs of licensing musical performances would have remained insuperable.

Justice Holmes's faith in the ability of private institutions to establish ground rules for compensation had little effect on Congress, which resisted the extension of copyright liability against the technologies that succeeded radio—photocopying, cable television, home audiotaping and videotaping. Courts have been equally shortsighted. The Supreme Court should have realized that, even if it had ruled for Universal and Disney rather than for Sony in the Betamax case, the film companies would not have sought injunctions against home copiers. More likely, working together with VCR manufacturers, the studios would have negotiated a VCR and videotape royalty that reflected the value of VCRs and video-cassettes in making home recordings of copyrighted films.

Can the collective, pioneering spirit that motivated composers, authors, and publishers to form ASCAP in 1913 survive in the last jaded years of the century? At least in the case of photocopying, the answer appears to be yes. In the mid-1970s, a spirited cadre of publishers organized the Copyright Clearance Center to collect photocopying royalties. Its work shows how congressional timidity about extending copyrights can hamper institutional efforts to reduce transaction costs, and how bold thinking can enhance them. The Copyright Clearance Center may have lacked William Passano's iconoclastic temperament, but it had a more ambitious plan than his proposed solution of a two-cent royalty for each copied page. Also, unlike Passano, it enjoyed early and widespread support in the publishing community and among writers.

The strategic decision to include writers on its board of directors at first hobbled the Center's efforts. The publishers wanted a cheap, blanket system like ASCAP's; the writers did not. Alexander Hoffman, a Doubleday vice president and the visionary who guided the Center's early years, recalled that the writers were afraid of "setting a precedent that would somehow or other diminish the ability of an individual creative writer to control his work." To keep them on board, the Center devised a Transactional Reporting System that would ensure that users paid for every work they copied. Publishers would print a legend at the bottom of the first page of their books indicating the fee to be paid for copies, and users would account for each copy made, periodically remitting the accumulated sums to the Center for distribution to its members.

However well this may have assuaged the writers' concerns, the service was a record-keeping nightmare. After signing up more than seven hundred users, the Center received reports from only fifty-five. The Transactional Reporting Service put a heavy burden on publishers as well. Reviewing his first royalty statement from the Center in 1978, William Passano did some quick arithmetic: "It costs us $.93 per article to place the CCC identification line on the first page of the articles published in our journals. The records show 2622 articles published in the first six months of 1978 and the cost of the CCC identification is therefore $2430 against an income of $732."

After three harrowing years, the Copyright Clearance Center was in a bind. If license revenues scarcely compensated publishers for the cost of participation, few would stay members and fewer still would join. Fewer members meant fewer works available for license, and a licensing service that offered only spotty coverage could hardly attract and retain the subscribers whose payments would support the enterprise.

Copyright's legal environment was also problematic. Section 108 of the new Copyright Act covered only library photocopying. Many nonlibrary users—including educators and businesses—read the *Williams & Wilkins* decision to hold that their activities constituted fair use and that they did not have to take a copyright license. Hoffman and his board understood that if the Center was to survive it would have to hold out both a carrot and a stick: the carrot would be a new low-cost licensing system that promised access to an extensive, even if not comprehensive, library of works; the stick would be an enforceable legal rule to the effect that unlicensed photocopying, in schools and offices as well as libraries, constituted copyright infringement.

ASCAP became the model for the Center's new licensing mechanism, the Annual Authorization Service. Under the new service, the Center would audit each user's photocopying activities on the user's premises and convert the results of the audit to a statistical model that accounted for the number of times the user copied the works of individual publishers. After each publisher specified an acceptable license fee for its works, the Center, using the audit-based statistical model, would figure the license fee it should collect from each user and the sums it should distribute to individual publishers. General Electric became the first subscriber to the service in October 1984 at a reported annual fee of more than $100,000.

Wielding the copyright stick required a carefully planned strategy of test cases. In their first string of lawsuits, the publishers won quick settlements from several "copy shops"— photocopy stores that produced anthologies of selections made by college professors from copyrighted books and assigned as required reading in class. In one widely publicized case, the publishers obtained a settlement agreement from New York University, several of whose faculty members had put together course readers reproduced through a local copy shop. (The case found Alan Latman on the other side of the photocopying fence. Latman had joined the NYU law faculty in 1976 and assisted the university's general counsel in negotiating with the publishers.) In the first copy-shop case to go to trial, *Basic Books v. Kinko's Graphics*, the court ruled against Kinko's fair use defense and the publishers ultimately obtained a $1.9 million settlement for damages and legal fees; Kinko's also agreed not to file an appeal.

The next major lawsuit, filed in May 1985, was against Texaco, which had earlier signed on to the Transactional Reporting Service but, Copyright Clearance Center officials believed, had substantially underreported the number of copies it had made. The lawsuit had dangerously much in common with Passano's unsuccessful suit against the United States government. Like NLM and NIH, Texaco had made single copies of journal articles for its employees' use; the employees were researchers, not pirates; only a small handful of claimed infringements were before the court; the publishers had not paid the authors for their articles; and the articles were scientific, factual works of the sort that often welcome fair use.

But the publishers had two distinctive facts weighing in their favor. Unlike NIH and NLM, Texaco is a commercial enterprise; under the formula the Supreme Court had devised in the Betamax case, this put Texaco to the hard task of showing that its activities did not commercially harm the publishers. Also, although the publishers' litany of lost revenues looked suspiciously like Passano's unsuccessful claim of lost subscriptions, the publishers were able to add an economic claim that Passano could not: revenues lost to the Copyright Clearance Center.

On July 23, 1992, a federal district court in Manhattan ruled for the publishers, relying heavily on the argument that the Copyright Clearance Center removed any excuse for unauthorized copying. Copyright opinions rarely invoke the jargon of microeconomics, but Judge Pierre Leval's *Texaco* decision was an exception. Observing that "a problem that has bedeviled the application of the copyright laws to the making of copies has been the transaction costs of arriving at a license agreement, when a small number of photocopies is made," Leval noted that "a two-dollar royalty might easily engender hundreds of dollars of transaction costs, consuming many wasted hours." Pointing to the CCC, however, he concluded that, "in this manner, private cooperative ingenuity has found practical solutions to what had seemed unsurmountable problems. Texaco can no longer make the same claims as were successfully advanced by the NIH to the Court of Claims in 1973."

The Copyright Clearance Center's carrot-and-stick strategy was working. Writing to members in August 1993, the Center estimated that 1993 royalty payments would exceed $17 million, nearly three times the amount paid out the previous year. Potential licensees, who had taken a wait-and-see attitude during the seven years of the *Texaco* litigation, were now signing on. More than three hundred and fifty corporations agreed to Annual Authorization Service licenses. Equally important, the CCC library available for licensing had grown dramatically; it now consisted of 1.5 million journals, books, magazines, and newsletters produced by more than eighty-six hundred foreign and domestic publishers.

Even as the Copyright Clearance Center was winning the battle to bring photocopies under license, a newer technology was maturing—electronic databases which could make texts instantly available to researchers—that could seriously undermine any need for the Center's services. Technologies exist today to enable copyright owners and users to negotiate individual licenses for electronically stored works at a cost lower even than the cost of administering the Center's blanket license. When a copyright owner deposits its works into some future electronic retrieval system, it will be able to attach a price tag to each work, listing its rates for different uses of the work. If the user decides to make a copy at the posted rate, the system will print it out and electronically charge his account.

The celestial jukebox may reduce the transaction costs of

negotiating licenses not only for complete works, such as journal articles, but for small fragments as well. Many electronic data-retrieval systems today price access to their databases in much the same way the telephone company charges for long-distance calls—the amount of time consumed by the subscriber's access. But while a time-based pricing mechanism will be adequate for relatively fungible data, it may fail to satisfy an entertainment company, which might justifiably fear that a user will need only a few seconds to strip the most valuable elements from its entire library of works. Nevertheless, technologies may emerge that will enable copyright owners to charge users differently according to the value of each element used.

The capacity of the celestial jukebox to post a charge for access, and to shut off service if a subscriber does not pay his bills, should substantially reduce the specter of transaction costs. As these costs dissolve, so, too, should the perceived need for safety valves such as fair use. Indeed, the economic logic of the celestial jukebox, when superimposed on the text of the Copyright Act, might produce a law that contains no exemptions from liability at all. Even if not repealed, these exemptions will atrophy as suppliers obligate their subscribers contractually to pay for now exempted uses of copyrighted material.

One problem with this logic is that the celestial jukebox will not entirely displace traditional copyright markets, where exemptions will still be needed. Also, some of the 1976 Act's exemptions are there, not because of transaction costs, but because certain uses and users serve socially valuable ends. The statutory exemption for classroom performances of copyrighted works in nonprofit educational institutions is one example. If copyright owners try to circumvent these copyright exemptions by contract—and there is every reason to expect they will—Congress will have to reconsider the distributional aspects of its copyright agenda and decide whether to outlaw such contracts or to grant direct cash subsidies to these users.

In the near future, before copyright owners are able to charge subscribers electronically for every use of their works, courts will have to decide whether information networks such as Internet contributorily infringe copyright in contexts that Justice Holmes could not possibly have contemplated in the *Ben-Hur* case. In November 1993, a music publisher filed a class action copyright infringement lawsuit on behalf of more than one hundred and forty publishers against Compu-Serve, a major on-line computer service, claiming that it was a contributory copyright infringer because its computer bulletin board allowed subscribers to transmit digitally translated musical compositions to other subscribers without permission from the copyright owners. If it were to follow the line taken by other electronic bulletin board providers, CompuServe could have been expected to respond that it cannot exercise any greater control over the content of subscribers' messages than the postal service or the telephone company; but among its defenses was the argument that reproduction of musical works for "private use" does not infringe copyright. (Copyright litigation occupies a small legal world; Alan Latman's law firm defended CompuServe.)

The celestial jukebox will quickly become a global presence and will inevitably encounter protectionist measures aimed at shoring up the copyright balance of trade in importing countries. One early example is the decision of the French government to deny foreign film and record companies a share of the videotape and audiotape levies attributable to the copying of their works, and to subsidize domestic cultural activities with a portion of these levies. Other stratagems can be expected as nations seek to skim copyright revenues from the celestial jukebox.

In some cases, nations importing signals from the celestial jukebox will structure protectionist measures in terms of copyright and neighboring rights. In other cases, they will try to block the importation of foreign works more directly. In 1989, the European Community, as it was then called, adopted a directive requiring its member states to impose a 49.9 percent ceiling on non-European (principally American) broadcast content. The avowed ground was that this was necessary to maintain the integrity of European culture. In 1993, Ted Turner, still mired in the *Asphalt Jungle* dispute, confronted yet another facet of French chauvinism when he launched the Cartoon Network Channel in Europe, broadcasting cartoons from his extensive film library almost exclusively. The French were not amused, and refused him a license for cable transmission.

Such obviously protectionist measures as the European Broadcast Directive and France's subsidies to its film producers taken from foreign film revenues come more directly within the international trade process than within international copyright treaties. The central international trade arrangement is the General Agreement on Tariffs and Trade, which developed in 1947 out of efforts to restore order to postwar markets by reducing tariffs and other protectionist barriers. By 1993, one hundred and sixteen countries had agreed to the principles of GATT. After seven successive rounds of multilateral negotiations aimed at expanding GATT's reach, the United States, concerned over billions of dollars lost to intellectual property pirates, succeeded in expanding the agenda of the eighth set of GATT negotiations, the Uruguay Round, to include intellectual property.

The Broadcast Directive and the question of subsidies to domestic cultural industries were among the last stumbling blocks in the way of the Uruguay Round's December 15, 1993, deadline. France took the lead for the European Union, adamantly resisting American demands for the removal of quotas and subsidies. After several rebuffs, the United States negotiators, who were at this point taking their cue from the American entertainment industry, fell back on the same strategy that had served that industry in dealing with Congress at home: conceding the battle over existing technologies and focusing instead on future technologies that had not yet attracted entrenched constituencies. "We gave the French and the E.C. a very moderate proposal," said Jack Valenti, president of the Motion Picture Association of America. "We said keep your quotas, keep your subsidies, but allow the new technology to come in and be available to the citizens of Europe. We mean pay-per-view, video-on-demand, satellite delivery, digital, optical fiber, all the ways these programs will be delivered." But, he reported, the compromise "was rejected out of hand."

In a December 15 letter to Congress, President Clinton stated: "With regard to entertainment issues, we were unable to overcome our differences with our major trading partners, and we agreed to disagree. We will continue to negotiate, however, and until we reach a satisfactory agreement, we think we can best advance the interests of our entertainment industry by reserving all our legal rights to respond to policies that discriminate in these areas." In "reserving all our legal rights," the President was rattling the sword of unilateral trade sanctions that the United States might wield against countries that fail to protect American literary and artistic works.

Probably the most important feature of the Uruguay Round was its imposition of the Berne Convention's minimum economic standards on all GATT members. This step will, for the first time, give these standards an effective enforcement mechanism in the newly established World Trade Organization. The decision to do this suggests the measures that will be needed if copyright's goal of giving the public the widest variety of literary and artistic works at the lowest possible price is to be attained amid the clamor of the international trade bazaar, where rights in cultural products can readily be swapped for subsidies and tariffs on steel or rice. Just as the prescriptions for domestic copyright lawmaking—careful selection of subject matter, robust extension of rights—represent good policy for national economies, so Berne's similar prescriptions represent good policy for an international economy based on the principle of free trade.

The central object of free trade is to enhance prosperity worldwide by removing local tariffs and subsidies that raise the price of goods and services above their cost of production. One country's natural resources or manufacturing infrastructure may enable it to produce and export a certain good, such as steel, at a lower cost than another country; when a comparatively disadvantaged country imposes tariffs on imported steel in an effort to support its own steel industry, its citizens, forced to pay higher prices for steel products, will have less disposable income to spend on other products or services. Free trade aims to remove such blockages.

Copyright poses the same dilemma for the economics of international free trade as it does for the economics of domestic free markets: if society withholds copyright from literary and artistic works, writers, artists, and publishers can charge only very little for these works, if anything at all, with the result that their income, and consequently incentives to do more, will dwindle; but if society confers copyright, and prices rise, the works will reach smaller audiences, even though they could theoretically be disseminated to broader audiences at no additional cost.

Viewed in this light, the trade conflict between the United States and France over the French obligation to pay audiotape and videotape levies to American record and film producers looks very much like the conflict within the United States over the obligation of American consumers to pay for making private copies of American records and films. In both cases, the film and record companies argue that, as these private uses displace more traditional markets, the failure to compensate will reduce the possibilities for new motion pictures and sound recordings. American consumers—and the French government—will respond that the cost of producing new work has already been borne by purchasers in theaters and record stores, and since the new uses impose no additional burden, they should be allowed free of charge.

The parallels between the domestic and international economics of copyright suggest that the domestic prescription of extending copyright into every corner of economic value should apply in the international arena as well. If, as is more and more the case, producers aim at a worldwide market, this prescription will best ensure that the price mechanism gives them accurate signals of tastes around the world. It may also encourage production of specialized works, whose domestic audiences would not be large enough to support them, to reach markets all over the world. For example, a videotape of a Yiddish-language drama may attract too small an audience in the United States to justify the investment in its production. But when potential customers from around the world are added in, there may be more than enough revenue to support a high-quality production.

International copyright, no less than domestic copyright, will need to make expedient exceptions to the monolithic extension of rights. Transaction costs will continue to require exemptions in situations where collecting groups or electronic retrieval systems cannot reduce these costs to manageable levels. Exemptions or compulsory licenses for educational and research uses may also be needed to give countries all over the world the copyright breathing space they need to lift their people to levels of literacy and numeracy adequate to compete in the world marketplace. Here, too, parallels exist between domestic and international lawmaking. The concessions made for research and teaching uses in Third World countries following the 1967 Stockholm Protocol are roughly like the concessions that Congress made for library and educational uses in America's 1976 Copyright Act.

These limited exceptions to the prescription of extending rights worldwide have one fact in common: unlike concessions made for protectionist ends, they are integrally connected to the objects of copyright overall. Exemptions to accommodate transaction costs—on the principle that half a loaf is better than none—help to ensure the widest possible dissemination of literary and artistic works. Exemptions and compulsory licenses for research and educational uses recognize the transcendent claim these uses have on a copyright system whose founding premise is that a culture can be built only if toilers in the vineyard are free to draw on the works of their predecessors.

These prescriptions for international copyright fit comfort-

ably in the free trade framework. But they can expect to encounter resistance in countries that are less committed than is
the United States to the view that copyright should promote
the widest variety of literary and artistic expression at the
lowest possible cost. Some countries take the view that copyright is being used as a juggernaut for imported popular cultures that undermine domestic cultural traditions. Copyright's
stimulus to the expression of divergent political views may
threaten governments whose existence depends on the sup-
pression of dissident philosophies. And countries whose economic systems aim neither at free markets nor at consumer
welfare may simply reject any prescription that embodies
them as premises. The success of the prescriptions for international copyright will turn on their ability to answer these cultural, political, and economic arguments.

Carving out exemptions from copyright in order to
achieve domestic cultural objects, as France does by dipping
into audiotape and videotape levies to subsidize its own film
production, raises hard questions. So do the European
Union's quotas on broadcast content. If letting copyrighted
works from abroad seep into every corner of public life does
in fact deplete a local culture—in the same sense that removing the Elgin Marbles from the Parthenon to the British
Museum might be thought to have depleted Greek culture—constraints on copyright would deserve more than a
moment's pause. But it is far from clear that the infiltrating
foreign culture will displace domestic culture, or that any culture that cannot withstand the onslaught of a competing culture is worth preserving. There is also the nagging question
whether "cultural" measures are merely a façade for economic
protectionism. (More than cultural concerns may have lain
behind a lament of France's European Affairs Minister: "What

would remain of our cultural identity if audiovisual Europe consisted of European consumers sitting in front of Japanese television sets showing American programs?")

At bottom, cultural exemptions raise the question whether paternalism or consumer choice should rule a nation's culture. The two philosophies have coexisted for centuries. Although copyright developed in the eighteenth century as a market alternative to royal sources of centralized influence, it never completely displaced aristocratic or state patronage; the battles in the United States Congress over giving federal grants to difficult new art forms are just another chapter in the uneasy alliance between the two philosophies. Whether or not a rigorous copyright system means that Americans will listen to 2 Live Crew's "Pretty Woman" rather than read Thomas Jefferson, or that Frenchmen will watch *Jurassic Park* rather than read Voltaire, it seems unlikely that logic or experience will ever resolve the competing claims over a nation's culture.

Free markets for goods and free markets for ideas are closely, if not perfectly, entwined. Copyright has historically mediated between the two. Until the eighteenth century, European sovereigns kept communications under their thumbs, imposing monopoly and licensing controls on printing establishments in order to bar the spread of dissident views. But with the great revolutions of the eighteenth century came the political freedom and the commercial markets that, together with cheap printing, for the first time ensured writers that their work, their ideas, and their livelihood could be committed to the marketplace. It is no accident that the first copyright acts appeared at this moment in history. As Barbara Ringer has observed, "we know, empirically, that strong copyright systems are characteristic of relatively free societies."

As free markets displace centralized economies around the world, and to a lesser extent as politically open societies displace authoritarian. regimes, the market-based prescriptions for international copyright seem more likely to find a welcome reception than in the past. When the Soviet Union joined the Universal Copyright Convention in 1973, the step was at first hailed in the United States Congress as a "long overdue acceptance" of "responsibility toward authors and other creators of works distributed and performed in the Soviet Union." But the more studied, skeptical view was that Soviet adherence to the UCC was actually a ploy for its state-owned publishing company to expropriate the copyrights of dissident Soviet writers in order to suppress the circulation of their works abroad. (The 1976 Copyright Act invalidated such expropriations.) Less than twenty years later, American trade and copyright officials were actively negotiating copyright agreements with nations of the former Soviet bloc. In October 1992, China, long a copyright outlaw, signed the Berne Convention.

These developments in international copyright will doubtless win applause in the Office of the United States Trade Representative. But this is only because, at the moment, the United States is the world's leading copyright exporter. Trade balances shift. The United States was a net copyright importer in the nineteenth century and may well become one again in the twenty-first century, for it is entirely possible that the digital environment of the celestial jukebox will dissolve the magic that today makes American entertainment fare preeminent in world markets. Indeed, it may be a sign of changes to come that revenues from the sale of video games in the United States have exceeded motion picture box office receipts, and that the two companies dominating the video game market, Nintendo and Sega Enterprises, are Japanese. (The two companies were plaintiffs in copyright lawsuits that pitted them against American "pirates.")

The celestial jukebox, with its enhanced, worldwide access to the raw materials of literary and artistic creation and the means to craft them into new products, will reduce the infrastructure costs—printing plants, film studios, distribution channels—that presently exclude less developed economies from creating substantial copyright export industries. Barriers to copyright markets have always been quite low, which helps explain why even developing countries have followed the nineteenth-century Belgian example and honored foreign copyrights on the premise that importation of cheap copies is not the way to build a domestic copyright industry. The celestial jukebox promises to level the copyright playing field even more.

The celestial jukebox may also portend more revolutional changes in international copyright markets. As the celestial jukebox disseminates information and entertainment over the air and without regard for national boundaries, the importance of the nation-state as the traditional guarantor of copyright may be replaced by international institutions such as the newly established World Trade Organization. (In the early 1990s the European Community had to resolve the thorny question whether liability for satellite transmission of copyrighted works should be determined by the law of the country where the transmission originates or the law of the country where it is received.) The French decision in 1852 to extend copyright to all authors regardless of nationality may become the emblem of copyright's international future.

The celestial jukebox can also be expected to reduce, or at least change, the role of today's book publishers and motion picture and record producers, giving authors a more central place in the creation and distribution of literary and artistic works. Economies of scale in production facilities, in risk finance, and in distribution networks have long placed these institutions at the center of cultural life. But tomorrow's author, artist, or composer who has access to a networked computer—most will—can bypass not only these corporate entities but also libraries and retail outlets, to communicate directly with his intended audience. Electronic bulletin boards that now vibrate with exchanges ranging from the hottest industry gossip to the most popular new restaurant will soon evolve into pathways for disseminating more extended and complete new works.

Such direct, unedited communications will quickly swamp audiences—not only with scientific articles that have not been subjected to the rigors of peer review but with an undifferentiated mass of poetic musings, home movies, and basement band recordings. Some users may have the time to wade through this morass on their own. But most will want someone to screen this fare for them, much as book publishers and motion picture and record producers—and book reviewers, film critics, and radio stations—do today. Such selection, editing, and evaluation require substantial human effort. But, like the "sweat of the brow" that goes into collecting databases and writing computer programs, these efforts will rarely command copyright protection.

A December 1993 *New York Times* interview with Scott Adams, creator of the widely syndicated comic strip *Dilbert*, well expresses the direction that authorship will take in the age of the celestial jukebox. Adams put the life-or-death fate of one of his characters to a vote of his readers. Ballots cast on the worldwide Internet computer network spared the character, with a fifty-seven percent majority in his favor. "I got maybe 3,000 votes, but many probably got lost in bit heaven because my mail system cuts off at 500 messages a day," he said, adding, "This whole E-Mail thing has been a great boon. I get several good strip suggestions a day and use many of the situations they suggest."

The digital future is the next, and perhaps ultimate, phase in copyright's long trajectory, perfecting the law's early aim of connecting authors to their audiences, free from interference by political sovereigns or the will of patrons. The main challenge will be to keep this trajectory clear of the buffets of protectionism and true to copyright's historic logic that the best prescription for connecting authors to their audiences is to extend rights into every corner where consumers derive value from literary and artistic works. If history is any measure, the result should be to promote political as well as cultural diversity, ensuring a plenitude of voices, all with the chance to be heard.

Notes

Most of the cases referred to in the text are cited by their location in the West Publishing Company's National Reporter System, available in county law libraries as well as in law school libraries and many law offices. Federal District Court opinions are cited to the Federal Supplement (F. Supp.) and Circuit Court opinions to the Federal Reporter (F., F.2d or F.3d, depending on the date of decision). Supreme Court opinions are, where possible, cited to the official United States Reports (U.S.). References to federal legislation are to the United States Code (U.S.C.).

1

James Thomson's *The Seasons* figured in two landmark, eighteenth-century English decisions, *Millar v. Taylor* and *Donaldson v. Becket*; they are discussed in Chapter 2. "Literary Larceny" appears in Augustine Birrell, *The Law and History of Copyright in Books* 167 (1899).

The District Court decision in *Acuff-Rose Music Inc. v. Campbell* is reported at 754 F. Supp. 1150 (M.D. Tenn. 1991); Oscar Brand's statement is quoted in the Circuit Court opinion at 972 F.2d 1429, 1433 (6th Cir. 1992).

The Salinger lawsuit, *Salinger v. Random House, Inc.*, is reported at 811 F.2d 90 (2d Cir. 1987), and the Monty Python suit, *Gilliam v. American Broadcasting Cos.*, at 538 F.2d 14 (2d Cir. 1976). Justice Story's reflections on "the metaphysics of the law" appear in *Folsom v. Marsh*, 9 Federal Cases 342, 344 (C.C.D. Mass. 1841).

Alan Latman's observations on the confusion between copyright, patent, and trademark were made in the course of an August 1, 1970, speech to the American Bar Association Section on Patents, Trademarks, and Copyrights in St. Louis, Missouri; it is reprinted in 60 *Trademark Reporter* 506 (1970). The United States patent law is codified in 35 U.S.C. §§1 *et seq.* The constitutional source for the copyright and patent laws is U.S. Constitution, Art. 1, §8 cl. 8. Federal trademark law is codified in 15 U.S.C. §§1051 *et seq.*; its constitutional source is the Commerce Clause, U.S. Constitution, Art. 1, §8 cl. 3. For an example of a Disney lawsuit based on overlapping claims of copyright and trademark in character depictions—characters appearing in Disney's motion picture *Pinocchio*—see *Walt Disney Productions v. Filmation Assocs.*, 628 F. Supp. 871 (C.D. Cal. 1986).

The Johnny Carson case, *Carson v. Here's Johnny Portable Toilets, Inc.*, is reported at 698 F.2d 831 (6th Cir. 1983), and the Associated Press case, *International News Service v. Associated Press*, at 248 U.S. 215 (1918).

The role of African countries in the folklore protection movement is described in Marie Niedzielska, "The Intellectual Property Aspects of Folklore Protection," *Copyright* 339 (November 1980). The $4.94 million advance for *Scarlett* is reported in "Headliners: by the Pen," *New York Times*, May 1, 1988, Sec. 4, p. 7. The commentary by Jon Pareles appears in "Rappers in Court Over Parody, Not Smut, and It's Still a Hard Call," *New York Times*, November 13, 1993, Arts Sec. pp. 3, 18, and the letter to the editor from Edward Murphy appears in *New York Times*, December 3, 1993, Sec. A, p. 32.

Notes

The Court of Appeals decision in the 2 Live Crew case, *Acuff-Rose Music, Inc. v. Campbell*, is reported at 972 F.2d 1429 (6th Cir. 1992). The Hemingway case is *Hemingway v. Random House, Inc.*, 244 Northeastern Reporter 2d 250 (1968). The Copyright Act, 17 U.S.C. §§ 101 *et seq.*, dropped all remaining formalities as a condition to protection, effective March 1, 1989. For a somewhat dated but still very illuminating discussion of liability for idea submissions, see Harry ˙Olsson, "Dreams for Sale," 23 *Law and Contemporary Problems* 34 (1958).

The quotation from Oliver Wendell Holmes, Sr., appears in "Mechanism in Thought and Morals," in *Pages from an Old Volume of Life: A Collection of Essays, 1857–1881*, 288 (1883). The Copyright Act's fair use defense appears at 17 U.S.C. §107. The Howard Hughes case is *Rosemont Enterprises v. Random House, Inc.*, 366 F.2d 303 (2d Cir. 1966); the Zapruder film case is *Time, Inc. v. Bernard Geis Assocs.*, 293 F. Supp. 130 (S.D.N.Y. 1968); the *Nation* case is *Harper & Row Publishers v. Nation Enterprises*, 471 U.S. 539 (1985); and the Groucho Marx case is *Marx v. The United States*, 96 F.2d 204 (9th Cir. 1938). Section 506(a) of the Copyright Act imposes criminal liability on copyright infringement committed "willfully and for purposes of commercial advantage or private financial gain"; the 1992 amendment imposing the felony sanction appears at 18 U.S.C. 2319(b).

Stephen Breyer's essay "The Uneasy Case for Copyright: A Study of Copyright in Books, Photocopies, and Computer Programs" appears at 84 *Harvard Law Review* 281 (1970); Barry Tyerman's reply, "The Economic Rationale for Copyright Protection for Published Books: A Reply to Professor Breyer," at 18 *UCLA Law Review* 1100 (1971); and Breyer's reply to Tyerman, "Copyright: A Rejoinder," at 20 *UCLA Law Review* 75 (1972).

The differences—and similarities—between American copyright law and copyright in other countries, as well as the treaty arrangements that seek to unite them, are examined in Chapter 5. The reference to piracy of Agatha Christie mysteries and the *Gone with the*

Wind sequel in Russia appears in Gleb Uspensky and Peter B. Kaufman, "50 Million Agatha Christies Can be Wrong," *Publishers Weekly*, November 9, 1992, p. 60.

The figures on the contemporary growth of book publishing are from Charles Barber, "Books by the Number," 6 *Media Studies Journal* 15 (Summer 1992). Chapters 2, 3, 4, and 6 tell the story of copyright's encounters with new technologies, from photography through computer programs, in Congress and the courts. Section 106(4) of the Copyright Act limits copyright liability for performances to those that are "public"; section 101 of the Act defines "public performance."

WIPO's director general, Arpad Bogsch, raised the question "Who is the *author* of what *work*?" at a WIPO symposium held at Stanford University on March 25–27, 1991; the author served as general reporter for the symposium. The proceedings were published in World Intellectual Property Organization, *WIPO World-wide Symposium on the Intellectual Property Aspects of Artificial Intelligence* (1991).

Discussion of the "iron law of consensus" appears in Thomas Olson, "The Iron Law of Consensus: Congressional Responses to Proposed Copyright Reforms Since the 1909 Act," 36 *Journal of the Copyright Society* 109 (1989). The observation about "working on the cutting edge of technology" was made by Haines Gaffner and appears in *Proceedings of the Congressional Copyright and Technology Symposium, Fort Lauderdale, Florida, February 4–5, 1984,* Prepared at the Request of the Subcomm. on Patent, Copyright and Trademark for use of the Senate Comm. on the Judiciary, 99th Cong. 1st Sess. (S. Print 99–71, July 1985). (The author of this book served as general reporter for the symposium.) Subcommittee chair Robert Kastenmeier endorsed the view in an article he co-authored with his chief counsel, Michael Remington, "The Semiconductor Chip Protection Act of 1984: A Swamp or Firm Ground?," 70 *Minnesota Law Review* 417 (1985).

The contributions of Justice Oliver Wendell Holmes, Jr., to the

Notes

law of copyright are discussed in Chapter 2. The Supreme Court decision in the 2 Live Crew case is reported at 114 Supreme Court Reporter 1164 (1994). The quotation from Mattheson, translated by the author's colleague Leonard Ratner, appears in Johann Mattheson, *Der Vollkommene Kapellmeister: Das ist Gründliche Anzeige* (1739).

2

The references to Milton, Burke, Goldsmith, Mansfield, and Holmes are expanded later in the chapter; the Hersey reference is to his dissent from National Commission on New Technological Uses of Copyrighted Works, *Final Report* 27 (1978). The Martial reference appears in Bruce Bugbee, *Genesis of American Patent and Copyright Law* 13 (1967), and the reference to King Diarmid is in Augustine Birrell, *The Law and History of Copyright in Books* 42 (1899).

The description of Crown patents and licenses, the operation of the Stationers' Company, and the enactment of the Statute of Anne draws heavily on L. Ray Patterson, *Copyright in Historical Perspective* (1968), as well as on Bruce Bugbee, *Genesis of American Patent and Copyright Law* (1967); Thomas Scrutton, *The Law of Copyright* (4th ed., 1903); and Harry Ransom, *The First Copyright Statute* (1956). John Milton's assent to publication of *Paradise Lost* appears in 6 David Masson, *The Life of John Milton* 509–11 (1965). The citation to the Statute of Anne is 8 Anne, c. 19 (1710).

The discussion of the Stationers' litigation efforts, from *Tonson v. Collins* through *Donaldson v. Becket,* is drawn primarily from L. Ray Patterson, *Copyright in Historical Perspective* (1968), and Mark Rose, "The Author as Proprietor: *Donaldson v. Becket* and the Genealogy of Modern Authorship," 23 *Representations* 51 (1988) (this essay also appears in substantially expanded form in Mark Rose, *Authors and Owners: The Invention of Copyright* [1993]), as well as Howard

241

Notes

Abrams, "The Historic Foundation of American Copyright Law: Exploding the Myth of Common Law Copyright," 29 *Wayne Law Review* 1119 (1983); Benjamin Kaplan, *An Unhurried View of Copyright* (1967); and Augustine Birrell, *The Law and History of Copyright in Books* (1899).

The reference to attendance by Burke, Goldsmith, and Garrick is from Mark Rose, "The Author as Proprietor: *Donaldson v. Becket* and the Genealogy of Modern Authorship," 23 *Representations* 51–52 (1988), and the speculation about the miscount of the judges' vote in *Donaldson v. Becket* appears in Howard Abrams, "The Historic Foundation of American Copyright Law: Exploding the Myth of Common Law Copyright," 29 *Wayne Law Review* 1119, 1156–71 (1983).

The case citations are: *Millar v. Taylor*, 4 Burr. 2303, 98 Eng. Rep. 201 (K.B. 1769); *Donaldson v. Becket*, 4 Burr. 2408, 98 Eng. Rep. 257 (1774). Justice Mansfield's last observations on copyright appeared in *Sayre v. Moore* (1785), cited in a footnote to *Cary v. Longman and Rees*, 1 East 180, 102 Eng. Rep. 138 (K.B. 1801).

The discussion of copyright's early years in America is drawn generally from Bruce Bugbee, *Genesis of American Patent and Copyright Law* (1967); Barbara Ringer, "Two Hundred Years of American Copyright Law," in American Bar Association, *Two Hundred Years of English and American Patent, Trademark and Copyright Law* 117 (1977); and Walter Pforzheimer, "Historical Perspective on Copyright Law and Fair Use," in Lowell Hattery and George Bush, eds., *Reprography and Copyright Law* 18 (1964).

For additional background on Noah Webster's role, see Harry Warfel, *Noah Webster: Schoolmaster to America*, chap. IV (1936). James Madison's observation on the lack of uniformity in laws concerning literary property appears in *Federalist Paper* No. 43 (Modern Library ed., 1941), and the deliberations in the Constitutional Convention are reprinted in Max Farrand, ed., *II Records of the Federal Convention of 1787*, 509 (1911). The citation to the first American Copyright Act is Act of May 31, 1790, ch. 15, 1 Stat. 124.

Notes

The description of the personalities and events leading to *Wheaton v. Peters* is drawn from Craig Joyce, "The Rise of the Supreme Court Reporter: An Institutional Perspective on Marshall Court Ascendancy," 83 *Michigan Law Review* 1291 (1985). The citations to the case are *Wheaton v. Peters*, 29 Federal Cases 862 (C.C.E.D. Pa. 1832) and *Wheaton v. Peters*, 33 U.S. 590 (1834).

The citation to the 1870 Act is Act of July 8, 1870, ch. 230 §§86–111, 16 Stat. 198, 212–16. The history of the Library of Congress and the Copyright Office is drawn from John Cole, "Of Copyright, Men, and a National Library," 28 *Quarterly Journal of the Library of Congress* 114 (1971).

The citation to the *Uncle Tom's Cabin* case is *Stowe v. Thomas*, 23 Federal Cases 201 (C.C.E.D. Pa. 1853); to the 1865 copyright amendments, Act of March 3, 1865, ch. 126, 13 Stat. 540–41; to the Oscar Wilde photograph case, *Burrow-Giles Lithographic Co. v. Sarony*, 111 U.S. 53 (1884); and to the *Trade-Mark Cases*, 100 U.S. 82 (1879).

The case involving *The Autocrat of the Breakfast Table* is *Holmes v. Hurst*, 174 U.S. 82 (1899). The citations to Holmes's four copyright opinions discussed in this chapter are: *Bleistein v. Donaldson Lithographing Co.*, 188 U.S. 239 (1903) (the circus poster case); *Kalem Co. v. Harper Bros.*, 222 U.S. 55 (1911) (the *Ben-Hur* case); *White-Smith Music Publishing Co. v. Apollo Co.*, 209 U.S. 1 (1908) (the pianola roll case); and *Herbert v. Shanley Co.*, 242 U.S. 591 (1917) (the for-profit performance case). Holmes's taste for popular theater is described in Peter Gibian, "Opening and Closing the Conversation: Style and Stance from Holmes Senior to Holmes Junior," in Robert W. Gordon, ed., *The Legacy of Oliver Wendell Holmes* 190 (1992).

The trial court decision in the Edison motion picture case is *Edison v. Lubin*, 119 F. 993 (E.D. Pa. 1903); the appellate decision is *Edison v. Lubin*, 122 F. 240 (3rd Cir. 1903). The amendment to the Copyright Act covering movies is Act of Aug. 24, 1912, ch. 356, Pub. L. No. 62–303, 37 Stat. (part 1) 488–90.

Notes

The Aeolian Company's attempted monopoly is described in Hearings on S. 6330 and H.R. 19853, 59th Cong., 1st Sess., 23–26, 94–97, 139–48, 166, 185–98, 202–6 (June 6–9, 1906); H. Rep. No. 2222, 60th Cong., 2d Sess., pp. 7–8 (1909). The citation to the 1909 Copyright Act is Act of March 4, 1909, Pub. L. No. 60–349, 35 Stat. (part 1) 1075.

The testimony by Herbert and Sousa appears in Arguments before the Committees on Patents of the Senate and House of Representatives, Cojointly, on the Bills, S. 6330 and H.R. 19853, to Amend and Consolidate the Acts Respecting Copyright, June 6–9, 1906. The 1897 amendment granting a public performance right to musical compositions is Act of Jan. 6, 1897, ch. 4, 29 Stat. 481–82. The reference to SACEM's founding is from David Sinacore-Guinn, *Collective Administration of Copyrights and Neighboring Rights* §1.01 (1993).

The story of ASCAP is drawn mainly from Leonard Allen, "The Battle of Tin Pan Alley," *Harper's* 514 (October 1940); Raymond Hubbell, *The Story of ASCAP* (undated and unpublished; on file with ASCAP); and Lucia Schultz, "Performing-Right Societies in the United States," *Music Library Association Notes* 511 (1979).

The citation to the Hilliard Hotel case is *John Church Co. v. Hilliard Hotel Co.*, 221 F. 229 (2d Cir. 1915), and to the Shanley's case, *Herbert v. Shanley Co.*, 222 F. 344 (S.D.N.Y. 1915), *affirmed*, 229 F. 340 (2d Cir. 1916). The Supreme Court decision is reported at 242 U.S. 591 (1917). The Bamberger case is *M. Witmark & Sons v. L. Bamberger & Co.*, 291 F. 776 (D.N.J. 1923). The antitrust consent decrees are *United States v. Broadcast Music, Inc.*, 1940–43 Trade Cases (CCH) §56,096 (February 3, 1941); and *United States v. American Society of Composers, Authors and Publishers*, 1940–43 Trade Cases (CCH) §56,104 (March 4, 1941).

3

This chapter draws principally on three sources: interviews with William Passano, Sr. (Baltimore, Md., December 18, 1986), Martin Cummings (Chesapeake Beach, Md., May 20, 1991), and Arthur Greenbaum (New York, N.Y., March 7, 1988); the *Williams & Wilkins* litigation correspondence files in the possession of Cowan, Liebowitz & Latman, P.C., New York, N.Y.; and the transcripts of the trial and the Supreme Court arguments in *Williams & Wilkins v. The United States.*

Additional and confirming facts were drawn from interviews with Thomas Byrnes (Washington, D.C., June 26, 1990); James Davis (Washington, D.C., June 26, 1990); Charles Lieb (New York, N.Y., March 7, 1988); William Passano, Jr. (Baltimore, Md., December 18, 1986); Barbara Ringer (Washington, D.C., June 29, 1990); Dorothy Schrader (Washington, D.C., January 3, 1991); Carol Simkin (New York, N.Y., March 8, 1988). A March 10, 1994, letter from Robert Bork provided further information.

The portrait of Joseph da Passano is reproduced in the Passano family history, William Moore Passano, *A Mad Passano Am I* (1978). The *Washington Post* reference to the *Williams & Wilkins* case appears in John MacKenzie, "Photocopying Case Tops Supreme Court Business List," *Washington Post*, October 13, 1974, p. K1. Background information on the National Library of Medicine and on Martin Cummings is drawn from Wyndham Miles, *A History of the National Library of Medicine: The Nation's Treasury of Medical Knowledge* (1982).

Latman's fair use study is Alan Latman, "Fair Use of Copyrighted Works," in Studies Prepared for the Subcomm. on Patents, Trademarks, and Copyrights of the Senate Comm. on the Judiciary, 86th Cong., 2d Sess. Copyright Law Revision (Comm. Print 1960). The provision of the Judicial Code allowing copyright infringement suits against the U.S. government is 28 U.S.C. §1498. The studies on the quantity of photocopying in the 1960s are summarized in

Notes

U.S. Copyright Office, *Summary of the Three Leading Studies That Deal with Photocopying in the United States and Its Copyright Implications* (1968).

The citation to the Fortnightly case is *Fortnightly Corp. v. United Artists Television, Inc.*, 392 U.S. 390 (1968); to Commissioner Davis's decision, *Williams & Wilkins v. The United States*, 172 United States Patents Quarterly (BNA) 670 (Ct. Cl. 1972); to the Court of Claims decision, *Williams & Wilkins v. The United States*, 487 F.2d 1345 (Ct. Cl. 1973). The *Gaslight* decision is *Benny v. Loew's, Inc.*, 239 F.2d 532 (9th Cir. 1956), *affirmed by an equally divided Court sub. nom. Columbia Broadcasting System v. Loew's, Inc.*, 356 U.S. 43 (1958).

The Howard Hughes case is *Rosemont Enterprises, Inc. v. Random House, Inc.*, 366 F.2d 303 (2d Cir. 1966); the choral instructor case, *Wihtol v. Crow*, 309 F.2d 777 (8th Cir. 1962); and the TelePrompTer case, *TelePrompTer Corp. v. Columbia Broadcasting System, Inc.*, 415 U.S. 394 (1974). The Supreme Court's order in *Williams & Wilkins* appears at 420 U.S. 376 (1975).

4

This chapter draws on the *Williams & Wilkins* litigation correspondence files in the offices of Cowan, Liebowitz & Latman, P.C., in New York, N.Y., and on interviews with Thomas Brennan (Washington, D.C., June 29, 1990); Martin Cummings (Chesapeake Beach, Md., May 20, 1991); Richard Elliott (Washington, D.C., June 17, 1993); Robert Kastenmeier and Michael Remington (Washington, D.C., October 20, 1992); David Leibowitz (Washington, D.C., June 18, 1993); Arthur Levine (Washington, D.C., June 27, 1990); Charles Mathias (Washington, D.C., February 7, 1990); Barbara Ringer (Washington, D.C., June 29, 1990); Harold Schoolman (telephone interview, March 9, 1994); Dorothy Schrader (Washington, D.C., January 3, 1991); Gary

Notes

Shapiro (Washington, D.C., August 16, 1993); and Robert Wedgeworth (Washington, D.C., July 12, 1993).

The statistics on ownership of videocassette and audiocassette recorders are from Gillian Davies and Michèle Hung, *Music and Video Private Copying: An International Survey of the Problem in the Law* 28–29 (1993). The OTA survey is Office of Technology Assessment, *Copyright & Home Copying: Technology Challenges the Law* 3, 145–46 (1989).

The discussion of the history of efforts to revise the 1909 Act draws in part on Jessica Litman, "Copyright Legislation and Technological Change," 68 *Oregon Law Review* 275 (1989). The citations to the House and Senate Reports on the 1976 Act are H.R. Rep. No. 94–1476, 94th Cong. 2d Sess. 65, 71–72 (1976), and S. Rep. No. 94–473, 94th Cong. 1st Sess. 66 (1976). The Kazen–Kastenmeier colloquy appears at 117 Congressional Record 334, 748–49 (1971). Latman's fair use study is Alan Latman, "Fair Use of Copyrighted Works," in Studies Prepared for the Subcomm. on Patents, Trademarks, and Copyrights of the Senate Comm. on the Judiciary, 86th Cong., 2d Sess. Copyright Law Revision 11–12 (Comm. Print 1960).

The quotation from Register Kaminstein appears in House Comm. on the Judiciary, 89th Cong., 1st Sess., Copyright Law Revision, Part 6, Supplementary Report of the Register of Copyrights on the General Revision of the U.S. Copyright Law: 1965 Revision Bill 26, 28 (Comm. Print 1965). The decision for Barbara Ringer in her lawsuit against the Librarian of Congress is *Ringer v. Mumford*, 355 F. Supp. 749 (D.D.C. 1973). The CONTU report is National Commission on New Technological Uses of Copyrighted Works, *Final Report* (1978).

The author served as a consultant to plaintiffs' counsel in the Betamax case. The description of the Betamax litigation and the related legislative strategies draws in part on James Lardner, *Fast Forward* (1987). The District Court decision in *Universal City Studios, Inc. v. Sony Corp. of America* is reported at 480 F. Supp. 429 (C.D.

Cal. 1979); the Court of Appeals decision is reported at 659 F.2d 963 (9th Cir. 1981); and the Supreme Court decision at 464 U.S. 417 (1984).

The statistics on VCR sales in 1979–82 come from Electronic Industries Association, *The U.S. Consumer Electronics Industry in Review*, 1992 ed. The observation about congressmen "being realists" was made by James Lardner in *Fast Forward* 240 (1987). The references to the memoranda and draft opinions of the Justices in the Betamax case all draw on the Supreme Court papers of Justice Thurgood Marshall housed in the Library of Congress. The figure on the number of American homes with VCRs comes from Gillian Davies and Michèle Hung, *Music and Video Private Copying: An International Survey of the Problem in the Law* 29 (1993).

Some of the background information on digital audio recording is drawn from Office of Technology Assessment, *Copyright and Home Copying: Technology Challenges the Law* (1989). Judge Ferguson's observation on a device "to jam the unjamming of the jam" is reported in James Lardner, *Fast Forward* 119–20 (1987). The citation to the Audio Home Recording Act is Pub. L. No. 102–563, 106 Stat. 4237 (1992). The discussion of the public lending right is drawn from John Cole, "Public Lending Right," 42 *Library of Congress Information Bulletin* 427 (December 12, 1983), and John Sumsion, *Setting Up Public Lending Right: Report* (1984).

5

The description of Ted Turner's MGM transactions is drawn from Maurine Christopher, "Tracking the TBS-MGM Deal No Easy Task," *Advertising Age*, February 10, 1986, p. 54, Stratford P. Sherman and Wilton Woods, "Ted Turner: Back from the Brink," *Fortune*, July 7, 1986, p. 24, and "Ted Turner May Sell Assets to Pay for MGM/UA," *Los Angeles Times*, May 7, 1986, Business Section, p. 2. The observation on moral right securing "the intimate

Notes

bond" is in Raymond Sarraute, "Current Theory on the Moral Right of Authors and Artists Under French Law," 16 *American Journal of Comparative Law* 465 (1968).

The Henri Rousseau case is *Bernard-Rousseau v. Soc. des Galeries Lafayette*, Judgment of March 13, 1973 (Tribunal de la grande instance, Paris 3e), and is described in John Henry Merryman, "The Refrigerator of Bernard Buffet," 27 *Hastings Law Journal* 1023 (1976). The Gephardt moral right bill is H.R. 2400, 100th Cong., 1st Sess. (1987). Turner's comment, "I think the movies look better in color . . ." is quoted in Stephen Farber, "The Man Hollywood Loves to Hate," *Los Angeles Times Magazine*, April 30, 1989, p. 9.

The La Cinq case is reported as Judgment of May 28, 1991, Cass. civ. 1re, 1991 La Semaine Juridique (Juris-Classeur Périodique), and the description of it is drawn from Paul Geller, "French High Court Remands Huston Colorization Case," *New Matter* 1 (State Bar of California Intellectual Property Section) (Winter 1991–92), and Jane Ginsburg and Pierre Sirinelli, "Authors and Exploitations in International Private Law: The French Supreme Court and the Huston Film Colorization Controversy," 15 *Colum.-VLA J.L. & Arts* 135 (1991). A translation of the decision appears as an appendix to the Ginsburg-Sirinelli article.

The West German home taping case is described in Juergen Weimann, "Private Home Taping Under Sec. 53(5) of the German Copyright Act of 1965," 30 *Journal of the Copyright Society* 153 (1982). The observation on moral right by Recht appears in Pierre Recht, *Le Droit d'Auteur, Une Nouvelle Forme de Propriété: Histoire et Théorie* 281 (1969), as translated in Russell DaSilva, "Droit Moral and the Amoral Copyright: A Comparison of Artists' Rights in France and the United States," 28 *Bulletin of the Copyright Society* 1, 7 (1980). Jane Ginsburg's study is "A Tale of Two Copyrights: Literary Property in Revolutionary France and America," 64 *Tulane Law Review* 991 (1990).

The history of economic thought about copyright draws substantially on Gillian Hadfield, "The Economics of Copyright: An

Notes

Historical Perspective," 38 *Copyright Law Symposium* 1 (ASCAP) (1992). Smith's analysis appears in Adam Smith, *Lectures on Jurisprudence* 83 (1762) (R. Meek, D. Raphael, and P. Stein, eds., 1978), and Bentham's in Jeremy Bentham, "A Manual of Political Economy," in 3 *Works of Jeremy Bentham* 31, 71 (1839) (Jay Bowring, ed., 1962).

Macaulay's speech appears in Thomas Babington Macaulay, *Prose and Poetry* 731, 733–37 (G. Young, ed., 1967). Arrow's essay is Kenneth Arrow, "Economic Welfare and the Allocation of Resources for Invention," in NBER, *The Rate and Direction of Inventive Activity: Economic and Social Factors* 609 (1962). The Demsetz essay is Harold Demsetz, "Information and Efficiency: Another Viewpoint," 12 *Journal of Law and Economics* 1 (1969). For an illuminating contemporary essay on copyright economics, see William Landes and Richard Posner, "An Economic Analysis of Copyright Law," 18 *Journal of Legal Studies* 325 (1989).

The history of French–Belgian copyright relations is drawn from 1 Stephen Ladas, *The International Protection of Literary and Artistic Property* 25–26 (1938), and Sam Ricketson, *The Berne Convention for the Protection of Literary and Artistic Works: 1886–1986* 17–22 (1987). The history of the international copyright debate in the United States draws on James Barnes, *Authors, Publishers and Politicians: The Quest for an Anglo-American Copyright Agreement, 1815–1854* (1974). The description of the origins of the Berne Convention draws on Sam Ricketson, *The Berne Convention for the Protection of Literary and Artistic Works: 1886–1986*, Part I. The citation to the Chace Act is Act of March 3, 1891, ch. 565, 26 Stat. 1106.

Secretary Baldrige's testimony appears in U.S. Adherence to the Berne Convention: Hearings on H.R. 1623 Before the Subcomm. on Courts, Civil Liberties, and the Administration of Justice of the House Comm. on the Judiciary, 100th Cong., 1st Sess. 117 (1987). Dr. Bogsch's testimony appears in The Implications, Both Domestic and International, of U.S. Adherence to the International Union for the Protection of Literary and Artistic Works: Hearings before

Notes

the Subcomm. on Patents, Copyrights and Trademarks of the Senate Comm. on the Judiciary, 99th Cong., 1st Sess. 8 (1985).

The description of events surrounding the Stockholm Protocol draws on several sources: Nora Tocups, "The Development of Special Provisions in International Copyright Law for the Benefit of Developing Countries," 29 *Journal of the Copyright Society* 402, 406–7 (1982); Charles Johnson, "The Origins of the Stockholm Protocol," 18 *Bulletin of the Copyright Society* 91, 92–93 (1970); Irwin A. Olian, Jr., "International Copyright and the Needs of Developing Countries: The Awakening at Stockholm and Paris," 7 *Cornell International Law Journal* 81, 95 (1974); Robert Hadl, "Toward International Copyright Revision: Report on the Meetings in Paris and Geneva, September 1970," 18 *Bulletin of the Copyright Society* 183 (1970). The Preamble to the Brazzaville Conference is reprinted in Royce Frederick Whale, *Protocol Regarding the Developing Countries* 10 (1968).

Dr. Ficsor's testimony appears in "Questions Concerning National Treatment in Respect of a Possible Protocol to the Berne Convention," Hearings Before the Subcomm. on Intellectual Property and Judicial Administration of the House Comm. on the Judiciary, 103d Cong., 1st Sess. (1993). Robert Hadl's testimony appears in "A Possible Protocol to the Berne Convention (National Treatment)," Hearings Before the Subcomm. on Intellectual Property and Judicial Administration of the House Comm. on the Judiciary, 103d Cong., 1st Sess. (1993). The description of the French home taping law draws on André Lucas and Robert Plaisant, "France," in Paul Geller, *International Copyright Law and Practice* §9(2)(b).

6

The author claims credit neither for the celestial jukebox metaphor nor for any success in tracking down the creative mind that coined the term. Cary's observation on copyright registration for computer programs comes from George Cary, "Copyright Registration and Computer Programs," 11 *Bulletin of the Copyright Society* 362, 363 (1964). The 1879 Supreme Court ruling is *Baker v. Selden*, 101 U.S. 99 (1879).

The 1986 decision on the scope of copyright protection for computer programs is *Whelan Associates, Inc. v. Jaslow Dental Laboratory, Inc.*, 797 F.2d 1222 (3d Cir. 1986); the Second Circuit decision on scope of protection is *Computer Associates International, Inc., v. Altai, Inc.*, 982 F.2d 693 (2d Cir. 1992). The *Apple* decision is *Apple Computer, Inc. v. Microsoft Corp.*, 799 F. Supp. 1006 (N.D. Cal. 1992) (the decision has been appealed to the Ninth Circuit Court of Appeals), and the *Sega* decision is *Sega Enterprises, Ltd. v. Accolade, Inc.*, 977 F.2d 1510 (9th Cir. 1992) (the author was co-counsel to the American Committee for Interoperable Systems, which filed an *amicus curiae* brief in support of Accolade).

The District Court decision in *Feist* is *Rural Telephone Service Co., Inc. v. Feist Publications, Inc.*, 663 F. Supp. 214 (D. Kan. 1987); the Supreme Court decision is *Feist Publications, Inc. v. Rural Telephone Service Co., Inc.*, 499 U.S. 340 (1991).

The Patent Act's *sui generis* provisions for protecting plants and designs are 35 U.S.C. §§161–64 and §§171–73, respectively. The Semiconductor Chip Protection Act appears at 17 U.S.C. §901–14. The 1969 proposal for *sui generis* protection of computer programs appears in Elmer Galbi, "Proposal for New Legislation to Protect Computer Programming," 17 *Bulletin of the Copyright Society* 280 (1969).

The description of the origins and operations of the Copyright Clearance Center draws in part on interviews with Charles Ellis and Richard Rudick (New York, N.Y., March 8, 1988); Alexander Hoffman (New York, N.Y., March 8, 1988); Charles Lieb (New York, N.Y., March 7, 1988); and Ben Weil (New York, N.Y., March 8, 1988).

The settlement agreement in the NYU case is reprinted in Jon

Notes

Baumgarten and Alan Latman, eds., *Corporate Copyright and Information Practices* 167 (1983). The *Kinko's* case is *Basic Books, Inc. v. Kinko's Graphics Corp.*, 758 F. Supp. 1522 (S.D.N.Y. 1991); the settlement terms appear in Claudia MacLachlan, "Newsletter and Book Publishers Attempt Copyright Crackdown," *National Law Journal*, November 18, 1991, p. 10. The *Texaco* case is *American Geophysical Union v. Texaco, Inc.*, 802 F. Supp. 1 (S.D.N.Y. 1992) (the decision has been appealed to the Second Circuit Court of Appeals).

The Broadcast Directive is Council Directive 89/552/EEC, 1989 O.J. (L 298) 23. Ted Turner's problems with the Cartoon Network Channel are reported in Scott Kraft, "Culture Clash: New Turner Network Is Galling the French," *Los Angeles Times*, September 25, 1993, p. D1. The observation by Jack Valenti is quoted in Bernard Weinraub, "Clinton Spared Blame by Hollywood Officials," *New York Times*, December 16, 1993, p. D1. The observation by France's European Affairs Minister, Edith Cresson, is quoted in Jeannine Johnson, "In Search of . . . The European T.V. Show," 291 *Europe* 22 (November 1989). The observation on copyright and free societies appears in Barbara Ringer, "Two Hundred Years of American Copyright Law," in American Bar Association, *Two Hundred Years of English and American Patent, Trademark and Copyright Law* 117, 118 (1977), and the observations on Soviet adherence to the UCC in 119 Congressional Record 9387 (1973).

The comparative figures on video games and box office receipts are from Rick Tetzeli, "Videogames: Serious Fun," *Fortune*, December 27, 1993, p. 110. The article on "Dilbert" is Peter Lewis, "Dilbert's Creator Espouses the Interactive Lifestyle," *New York Times*, December 5, 1993, Sec. 3, p. 12.

Index

255

Index

Index

Index

Index

Index

patent law, 9–10, 20, 52, 95, 200–1, 203–4
Patent Office, U.S., 2–4, 211
Perkins, Eben, 85, 86, 90
Peters, Richard, 53–56
Peters' Reports, 55
photocopying, 22, 24, 29, 79–128; by libraries, 79–128, 134–43, 170; private, 116, 118, 130; royalties on, 219–23
photography, 58–60, 62, 192–93
Pitney, Mahlon, 13–14
plagiarism, 12, 39
Powell, Lewis, 151, 154
printing press, 39–41
private papers, 6–7, 18
private use, 116, 118, 123–24, 129–64, 169–70, 172, 217; audiotaping, 157–63; digital technology and, 201; French laws on, 194, 229; photocopying, 116, 118, 130, 134–43; videotaping, 143–58, 169
Protocol Regarding Developing Countries, *see* Stockholm Protocol
public domain, 14–16
Public Health Service, 90, 91
publicity, right of, 12

Recht, Pierre, 171
Recording Industry Association of America, 159, 162
Register of Copyrights, 188
Rehnquist, William, 124, 154–56
Reinhardt, Stephen, 210
Reville, Charles, 108, 142
Ringer, Barbara, 112, 135, 138–39, 141–43, 232
Roach, John, 162
Rogers, Fred, 145, 156
Rome Convention for the Protection of Performers, Producers of Phonograms and Broadcasting Organizations, 193, 194
Romeo and Juliet (Shakespeare), 205
Rosemont v. Random House Inc. (1966), 116–17
Rousseau, Henri, 166

Salinger, J. D., 6–7
Sarony, Napoleon, 58–60, 76
Saturday Night Massacre, 119
Scarlett, 15, 27
Schoolman, Harold, 113, 142
Seasons, The (Thomson), 4, 47–49, 56
Sega Enterprises, 209–11, 234
Semiconductor Chip Protection Act (1984), 215–16
Senate, U.S., 33, 81, 137, 140, 142, 148, 149, 151; Judiciary Committee, 119; Patent, Trademark, and Copyright Subcommittee, 96–97
Serial Copy Management System (SCMS), 160–63
Shanley's Restaurant, 69–70, 76, 218
Sherman Antitrust Act, 75
Simkin, Carol, 116, 126–27
Smith, Adam, 173–74, 176
Société des Auteurs, Compositeurs et Editeurs de Musique (SACEM), 68
Solberg, Thorvald, 56
Sony Corporation of America, 144–46, 149, 152–53, 159, 161, 210, 218
Sony v. Universal (1984), 149–58, 169, 170, 211
Sound Recordings Fund, 162–63
Sousa, John Philip, 67, 69, 70
Souter, David, 34
Soviet Union, 27, 232
Spofford, Ainsworth Rand, 56
Springsteen, Bruce, 202
Stationers' Company, 41–46, 50, 51, 56, 173
Statute of Anne, 43–45, 47, 49–51, 200
Stevens, John Paul, 149–52, 154–57
Stewart, Potter, 114
Stockholm Protocol, 188–89, 230
Story, Joseph, 9, 18, 84
Stowe, Harriet Beecher, 57
sui generis legislation, 215–16
Supreme Court, U.S., 13, 17, 21, 22, 33–34, 53–55, 58–61, 64–67, 70, 82, 89, 90, 92, 111–21, 123–27, 133, 134, 140, 149, 150, 152, 155, 157, 158, 169, 212–13, 216, 222
"Sweethearts" (Herbert), 69–70

Index